MW00413852

CREATIONISM AND THE CONFLICT OVER EVOLUTION

Cascade Companions

The Christian theological tradition provides an embarrassment of riches: from scripture to modern scholarship, we are blessed with a vast and complex theological inheritance. And yet this feast of traditional riches is too frequently inaccessible to the general reader.

The Cascade Companions series addresses the challenge by publishing books that combine academic rigor with broad appeal and readability. They aim to introduce nonspecialist readers to that vital storehouse of authors, documents, themes, histories, arguments, and movements that comprise this heritage with brief yet compelling volumes.

TITLES IN THIS SERIES:

Reading Augustine by Jason Byassee

Conflict, Community, and Honor by John H. Elliott

An Introduction to the Desert Fathers by Jason Byassee

Reading Paul by Michael J. Gorman

Theology and Culture by D. Stephen Long

Creationism and the Conflict over Evolution by Tatha Wiley

Justpeace Ethics by Jarem T. Sawatsky

Reading Bonhoeffer by Geffrey B. Kelly

FORTHCOMING TITLES:

Theological Interpretation of Scripture by Stephen E. Fowl

Christianity and Politics in America by Chad C. Pecknold

iPod, YouTube, Wii Play by D. Brent Laytham

Philippians in Context by Joseph H. Hellerman

CREATIONISM
and the Conflict over Evolution

TATHA WILEY

CASCADE *Books* • Eugene, Oregon

CREATIONISM AND THE CONFLICT OVER EVOLUTION

Cascade Companions

Cascade Books
A Division of Wipf and Stock Publishers
199 W. 8th Ave., Suite 3
Eugene, OR 97401

www.wipfandstock.com

ISBN 13: 978-1-55635-291-1

Cataloging-in-Publication data:

Wiley, Tatha.

Creationism and the conflict over evolution / Tatha Wiley.

x + 154 p.; cm. Includes bibliographical references.

Cascade Companions

ISBN 13: 978-1-55635-291-1

1. Creationism. 2. Evolution (Biology). 3. Evolution (Biology)—Religious aspects—Christianity. 4. Religion and science. I. Title. II. Series.

BL262 W54 2009

Manufactured in the U.S.A.

For Marion and Terry,
whose minds and achievements
are complemented by humor and deep hearts

Contents

Abbreviations

Adv. haer.	Irenaeus, *Adversus haereses* (Against Heresies)
B.C.E.	Before the Common Era
ca.	circa (approximately)
C.E.	Common Era
d.	died

Introduction

Who can gaze at a star-filled sky or breathe deeply of crisp mountain air without the feeling that we are part of a marvelous and mysterious universe? Our understanding of what we experience takes us from the spontaneity of feeling into the conceptual worlds of both religion and science. How do our current notions of the workings of the universe fit with our deepest convictions about its meaning and value? From religion, we grasp the world as created, given, gift. From science, we apprehend it as evolving, in process, changing. How do we bring these apprehensions together? Or can we? Is our impulse to find the two complementary: creation *and* evolution? Or is it to find them contradictory: creation *or* evolution?

The way we answer these questions has personal and intellectual consequences. It will constitute the first piece in a worldview within which we order our religious beliefs and scientific judgments.

PROBLEMATIC PRESUMPTIONS

When creation and evolution are thought to be incompatible, three problematic presumptions are often at work:

1. by *creation* is meant the biblical story of creation in Genesis 1, understood as a historical event,

2. Genesis 1 and evolutionary theory each describe the way the world began, and

3. we must choose between them.

If these presumptions are indeed at work, then we have engaged this controversy in terms shaped by fundamentalists, the most conservative of Christian traditions. If we take conflict and rivalry as givens, we have appropriated the fundamentalist understanding of creation. In fact, if we place creation and evolution against one another as alternatives, we have affirmed as real a conflict created by fundamentalists themselves.

Uncovering these presumptions and the misunderstanding of both creation and evolution that they impose is the chief purpose of this book. The debate between religion and science on the world's origins need not—indeed, should not—be dictated by the views of fundamentalists and creationists, the common designations for those who oppose evolutionary theory most vigorously. Fundamentalists are conservative Christians of various denominations. "Creationists" are fundamentalists whose public opposition to evolution includes attempts to persuade local and state school boards to eliminate evolutionary theory from science courses or to balance such theory with what they propose as the biblical view of the world's origins. We will define each more fully in the chapters ahead.

One misunderstanding is important to clarify right at the beginning. What fundamentalists mean by "creation" is Genesis 1 as revealed history, that is, an account of what God did in creating the physical universe. That is not the meaning of creation in the theological tradition. We will explore that meaning in chapter 2. Here it will suffice to say that the concept of creation does *not* refer to Genesis 1, nor does it compete with evolutionary theory as an account of the origin of species. As a theological concept, creation does not explain physical things, as evolution does, but answers the metaphysical question why there are physical things at all, a question that evolutionary science does not take up. With that said, we have already stepped out of the framework shaped by fundamentalists and into one in which our religious and scientific worldviews can integrate creation and evolution without conflict.

OBJECTIVES

The chief objective of this book is to move the debate about creation and evolution from a framework shaped by unnoticed fundamentalist presuppositions and conclusions to a historically conscious and scholarly framework in which we have an intelligent grasp of each of the components involved—the Bible, Christian doctrine, evolutionary science, and creationism. The following chapters address each of these components.

To shift frameworks requires separating creation from creationism. We have not done so if we hear the question, "Do you believe in creation?" as "Do you believe the events narrated in Genesis 1 really happened?" Rightly understood, creation and evolution are different realities in the order of being and different explanations in the order of knowing.

They are not competing answers to the same question but complementary answers to different questions.

A second objective is to bring the human desire to understand the world into focus. This desire is open and unrestricted.[1] It is expressed in the everyday understanding of living, the insight of the poet, and the technical analysis of the economist. Scientific inquiry is this desire on the move. The insights generated by inquiry become the building blocks of an explanatory knowledge of physical reality. But science does not fulfill the whole of the human desire to know. There are many questions science does not answer—questions about the meaning of texts and the value of art, for example.

Some questions are about the physical universe, but they are different than asking what happens to a flower as it grows. Why is there anything at all? What accounts for the intelligibility of the world, that is, the fact that it can be understood? What would account for contingent being? These are questions about the world, but they are *meta*-physical rather than physical questions. They are genuine questions, and anyone may engage them; but to do so is to do something other than science.

A third objective of this book is to unfold a progressive series of clarifications. From the side of theology especially, two clarifications are important. The first is to distinguish the Bible as understood by fundamentalists and the Bible as critically appropriated and fully informed by biblical scholar-

1. I am indebted to the work of Bernard J. F. Lonergan, SJ, for an understanding of human knowing in its development, structure, differences as common sense and theoretical, interferences, and so on. Of primary importance in his work are two major books: *Insight: A Study of Human Understanding* and *Method in Theology*.

ship. The latter is less evident in the creationist conflict over evolution than could be the case. When scientists and others argue with creationists, they not only talk about the Bible as fundamentalists do, but think that that is the way the Bible *is*. Christians in mainline traditions, for example, do not understand the biblical story of creation in the literalist way of fundamentalists. The fundamentalist understanding ignores the original historical context of the narrative, its writer, the purpose the writer had for it, its genre, and date of composition. That is a lot to ignore. To keep these kinds of factors in mind gives rise to a richer text without the contradictions with science that fundamentalists cannot avoid.

Moreover, the assertion that the Bible gives us complete historical and scientific truth—the idea of biblical inerrancy—is a reaction to and rejection of the emergence of historical-critical studies of the Bible. Mainline traditions take for granted the necessity of a scholarly appropriation of the Bible. Such factors as literary genre, historical context, and cultural milieu are important aspects of human meaning. As features of ancient texts they require the work of biblical specialists to unpack. A scholarly understanding of the story of creation in Genesis 1 puts an end to many pseudo-difficulties presented by fundamentalists. Chapter 1 takes up these topics.

We have suggested the nature of the second clarification already, one that we will deal with more fully in chapter 2. This is the clarification of the meaning of the theological concept of creation and the difference between this meaning and that given to creation by fundamentalists. The concept of creation, naturally, is the centerpiece of the doctrine of creation, a development that took place over the first several centuries of Christian history. In chapter 2, we will highlight the questions that engaged Christian theologians in the early centuries of the church. Are God and the world one? Are they distinct? Is matter eternal? Is the divine a personal or nonpersonal reality? What is the relation of the Creator to evil?

FURTHER TASKS

With these objectives and clarifications of the first two chapters, in the third chapter we introduce the outlines of the modern evolutionary theory. Among the key issues that generate fundamentalist resistance, we will treat:

- what Charles Darwin meant by natural selection as a mechanism of evolution and why that was an achievement;

- the nature of theory as scientific understanding;

- scientific method, the import of "bracketing God" as an explanation in scientific inquiry, and why this is legitimate from a theological point of view.

Here and elsewhere we will have the occasion to reject the fundamentalist claim that evolution is incompatible with God. Unless one reads Genesis 1 as an alternative to evolutionary theory, evolutionary theory is not a threat to faith but an unparalleled insight into the sheer magnificence of the universe. Scientists explain the world; they do not make it. What exists cannot be a surprise to the unrestricted understanding that grounds the intelligibility we discover.

In the following chapters, 4 and 5, we explore contemporary religious resistance to evolutionary theory. In chapter 4, we look at nineteenth- and early twentieth-century Catholic opposition. In chapter 5, we take up the current organized opposition of creationist groups, in particular young-Earth creationists and the Intelligent Design movement.

Chapter 6, the final chapter, addresses the question of why creationists engage in such resistance to evolution. Why is the historicity of Genesis 1 so important to them? What makes the historical truth of this story so crucial, so necessary, to fundamentalist faith? What is the consequence if Genesis 1 is not historical? Is the problem really creation?

Creationists face opposition from scientists worldwide. Why do they refuse evidence for evolution that scientists describe as overwhelming? What fear is so great that creationists would persist in their attempts to eliminate evolution not just from science courses but from our very minds? This refusal and fear are a real puzzle. Determining the reason that gives rise to this resistance and fear sheds light on the intellectual demands of authentic faith.

Eugenie Scott, Director of the National Center for Science Education, has written that education by both scientists and theologians is the solution to the problem of anti-evolutionism.[2] I hope this book contributes to the solution needed. But it is not only evolution that requires our attention. To deal with the controversy adequately we need to become informed about the Bible by biblical scholarship and about the doctrine of creation by historical and theological studies.

Opposition to evolution is not an abstract issue but a very concrete one of the human good. Science contributes not just abstract knowledge but also the means by which we meet the massive challenges of hunger, disease, and ecological dev-

2. Scott and Branch, "Antievolutionism: Changes and Continuities."

astation. We cannot hope for progress in the world without science. Scientists can go further than their methodological canons warrant and make pronouncements on transcendent reality and other matters. Such personal indiscretions are just boundary problems. Creationists do the same thing by trying to say they are doing science when they are pursuing a religious agenda.

But what creationists are doing when they threaten the integrity of science education carries serious consequences. Science is a condition for the possibility of the human good. Such a threat should be shown for what it is and resisted.

I am honored that this book will take its place in the Cascade Companions series. My thanks to Dr. K. C. Hanson, editor-in-chief of Cascade Books, for his friendship and invitation to take up this challenging topic. Corresponding to the series design and purpose, my treatment will be brief. Resources mentioned in the notes and bibliography provide suggestions for further reading.

I write as a Catholic theologian with a deep appreciation for the achievements of scientists and for the intellectual tradition of Christianity. My thinking about both is influenced by the work of Bernard Lonergan, SJ, whose insights into the structure of knowing are of particular value in understanding both the thinking of modern scientists and the oversights of religious fundamentalists.

ONE

The Bible and Creation

Christian fundamentalists have placed a particularly vulnerable understanding of the Bible at the center of the public debate about creation and evolution. They argue that the Bible is inerrant, true in its historical, scientific, and moral affirmations, without error or fault, to be believed and obeyed. It is normative for how we understand the world. If scientific conclusions are at odds with the Bible, it is the science that is to be rejected. They interpret the biblical story in Genesis 1 as the revelation of a historical event of divine creation.

The position of contemporary scientists on the world's origins and development is completely at odds with what fundamentalists assert about the Bible. From Genesis 1 fundamentalists infer the fixity of species, the creation of species by God essentially as they are today. In contrast, and from what they describe as overwhelming evidence, scientists argue that life has evolved over billions of years, with the incredible diversity and complexity of species that exists now having begun with single-cell microorganisms. In contrast to the fundamentalist appeal to the authority of the Bible as the basis of truth, scientists hold that what we know about the world is the product of judgments that are tested and verified by empirical research. Following literary critics, scientists would argue that the genre of Genesis 1 precludes it from scientific consideration. It is a symbolic narrative. The fixity of species and special creation are narrative details, not features of the world as it actually is.

The differences between the biblical position of fundamentalists and the evolutionary theory of scientists are reduced in common debate to a stark choice: either creation or evolution. Fundamentalists leave no room for anything other than this either/or choice. The choice is only necessary, however, because they insist on interpreting Genesis 1 as history. Moving out of the fundamentalist framework enables us to see that creation and evolution may not be exclusive alternatives at all. If we do not presume with fundamentalists that creation is equivalent to the account in Genesis 1, then creation and evolution are not rival descriptions of the world's origins. The alternative to the anti-modern and anti-intellectual understanding of the Bible, characteristic of conservative Christians, is a Bible understood through the many specialties of biblical scholarship. By appropriating key insights about the Bible from biblical scholars, we will be in a position to find the Bible and evolutionary science in a complementary rather than an adversarial relation.

WHAT IS THE BIBLE?

The Christian Bible is a complex book. As literary critics emphasize, the Bible is not *a* book, but many books. It is characterized more by difference than unity. The books are of different genres written by different authors in response to different problems, questions, and conflicts of different audiences at different times and places. Perhaps most elusive for later interpreters to discern, the authors had different purposes in writing.

Christians divide these sacred books into two "testaments." The Latin *testamentum* means covenant. The books are "Writings of the Covenant." The oral and written traditions of the Old Testament stretch over twenty centuries. Included in the Christian Bible are the thirty-nine writings of the Hebrew Bible considered canonical to Jews as well as some additional Jewish writings from ancient Israel that Catholics call deuterocanonical and Protestants call apocryphal. The writings reflect widely diverse cultural settings as well as a plurality of perspectives and purposes. A prophet who sees social reality through the lens of justice and injustice, for example, is quite different from the priest for whom ritual and cult are primary. One writer may be writing from within the context of military defeat and exile, another from the context of a royal court. Such are the radically different contexts for the first two creation stories in Genesis 1 and Genesis 2.

Composition of the twenty-seven New Testament writings took place in approximately half a century. Like the Hebrew Bible, these writings reflect multiple genres, authors, audiences, and locations. What separates them most decisively are their centers of attention. For the Hebrew Bible, the people and God of Israel are at the center. At the center of the New Testament is Jesus of Nazareth and his relationship to the God of Israel.

The individual New Testament books are differentiated by perspective as well. While one text advocates freedom and equality, another justifies slavery. The New Testament gospels offer not one portrait of Jesus, but four. Their accounts of Jesus' life are not records of the "events as they happened" but narratives written later to address problems, questions, and conflicts in each of their Jesus communities. Each of the four narratives builds upon historical memories of Jesus; but their intent is proclamation, not history. They want to communicate what the risen Jesus means to them, not simply what the historical Jesus said and did.

The Prologue of the Gospel of John opens with an obvious parallel to Genesis 1. Both books affirm a transcendent source for the universe. The Genesis story expresses this through a story in which God brings the universe into existence. In John, the focus is on the preexistence of Jesus who, as the divine Word, is the one through whom God creates:

> In the beginning was the Word,
> > and the Word was with God,
> > and the Word was God.
> He was in the beginning with God.
> All things came into being through him,
> > and without him not one thing came into being.
> > (John 1:1–3)

The two testaments share the biblical creation faith. The world is the choice of a loving God. For both testaments evil is a distortion of creation. The prophets denounce social injustice. The psalmist appeals to God to favor those sinned against, the dispossessed and excluded. Jesus announces God's favor for the poor and hungry. The social ethic of both testaments is grounded in the belief that creation is a *gift*. It expresses the love of the transcendent One whose ultimate power is revealed in the bestowal of existence. In its human realization, being comes with a moral imperative. The foundational principles are stated simply:

- Seek good and not evil, hate evil and love good
  (Amos 5:14, 15; Rom 12:9);

- Love the LORD your God with all your heart, and
  with all your soul, and with all your might (Deut 6:4;
  Matt 22:38);

- Love your neighbor as yourself (Lev 19:18; Matt
  19:19);

- Love your enemy (Luke 6:27; Rom 12:17).

- The God who is to be loved is one, creator of heaven
  and earth (Deut 6:4; Psalm 121; Col 1:16).

In both testaments the human problem is the distortion
that sin brings to creation. The solution is the love of God for
humankind that empowers humankind's fidelity to God. This
love grounds the communities oriented to God. As a way of
living, the Torah or Law orders life in relation to God. In the
New Testament, life is shaped by the model of Jesus. The apostle Paul sees redemption and reconciliation to God together
in the language of creation. Whoever is "in Christ" is a "new
creation" (2 Cor 5:17). By "in Christ" he meant in the Jesus
assembly. In rejecting the separation of Jews and Gentiles
signified by the mark of circumcision, he emphasized this
new unity: "For neither circumcision nor uncircumcision is
anything; but a new creation is everything!" (Gal 6:15).

THE DAWN OF MODERN BIBLICAL SCHOLARSHIP

"Modern" biblical scholarship is now several hundred years
old. Of course, Christians have always studied the Bible in-
tensely. The great theologians of the early church, such as

Jerome (d. 420 C.E.) and Augustine (d. 430 C.E.), contributed commentaries and translations, and they employed the Bible in their theological reflection.[1] Medieval theologians, such as Thomas Aquinas, lectured on biblical texts and developed techniques of interpretation. But unlike commentators in the tradition, whose interpretation tended to be in service of doctrine, the findings of modern scholars challenged traditional views about the Bible. They used critical historical and literary tools to understand the Bible, its context, composition, and historical reliability. Among their conclusions about the New Testament, for example, were such judgments as:

- the gospels circulated anonymously; authors' names were added later,

- Matthew and Luke used Mark's narrative for their own, changing his order and wording freely as they willed,

- not every word attributed to Jesus was actually spoken by him, and

- some of the letters attributed to Paul were written later by others.

Modern critical scholarship was first resisted as scandalous by Catholic and some Protestant churches, then accepted as necessary for understanding the texts. In the Catholic Church, Pope Leo XIII's 1893 encyclical, *Providentissimus Deus*—some forty years after Darwin's *Origin of Species*—

---

1. An account of modern biblical scholarship is given in "The Interpretation of the Bible: From the Nineteenth to Mid-Twentieth Centuries," and "Contemporary Methods in Biblical Study," in Coogan, ed., *The New Oxford Annotated Bible*, 491–505. See also Grant and Tracy, *The History of the Interpretation of the Bible*.

clarified that the Bible did not teach science and that what scientific views were expressed in the Bible reflected their cultural and historical setting. Fifty years later, the encyclical *Divino Afflante Spiritu* (1943), issued by Pope Pius XII, authorized the use of critical methods of inquiry by Catholic biblical scholars, confirming the necessity of scholarship for interpretation to be correct.[2]

This turn toward a more historically informed understanding is natural. But it is this move that separates fundamentalist from non-fundamentalist Christians. We will call the latter "mainstream" Christians for this comparison. Fundamentalism originated in the rejection of the whole range of modern developments, including historical-critical biblical scholarship. This rejection continues today. Their method of interpretation is personal and without engagement or concern for questions of authorship, context, historical background, genre, or sources. Whether the culture, way of thinking, or purpose of the author at the time of a writing is different from our own is irrelevant.

Both evolutionary science and biblical scholarship threatened the way in which the past was understood. This new historical sense had an impact on the understanding of texts such as Genesis 1–3. Were they to be read as symbolic narratives, not as history? Were Adam and Eve to be understood as prototypes, not as historical persons?

Fundamentalist Christians gave priority to the *concepts* in which the faith of the tradition has been formulated. For

2. Note also *Dei Verbum,* "The Dogmatic Constitution on Divine Revelation," in *The Documents of Vatican II* (1965); and the Pontifical Biblical Commission's publication, "The Interpretation of the Bible in the Church" (1994), online: http://www.ewtn.com/library/CURIA/ PBCINTER.htm.

faith to be retained, the concepts had to remain the same. Emerging facts about the world could not be admitted, nor could questions be entertained about doctrines. If our faith presumes the historicity of Genesis 1, for example, then the scientific story of evolution must be ruled out of court. The new situation that modernity presents through the sciences and history is not something to be engaged but something that must be resisted and rejected.

What has historical analysis told us about Genesis 1–3? The Hebrew Bible opens with the story of God's creating the universe over the course of six days and resting on the seventh day. *The* creation story usually means this one found in Genesis 1:1—2:4a. But read a further sentence (2:4b) and a second story immediately follows. It is obviously a creation story, too, but a very different one than the first one. We will look at Genesis 1 in terms of its genre, its purpose, and its context.

LITERARY GENRE

A genre is a kind of literary expression, and we are all used to reading many genres differently in our daily lives. We read letters and memos, journalistic reporting, fiction, and advertising. We bring a whole set of different expectations, degree of skepticism or credibility, to a cookbook than to a litany, or a weather report than an ad, a memoir than a short story, a poem than a bill.

As literary expression, Genesis 1 is best understood in terms of the genres of poetry and symbolic narrative. Literary critics call this kind of story *myth*. The way they understand that word, however, is different than the way it is used in common discourse. In ordinary language, *myth* means a commonly held but mistaken belief. But literary critics use *myth* to denote literary expressions—either poetic or narrative—that deal symbolically with fundamental questions. Why are we here? Is the universe good or bad? What is our purpose? There are several parallels to Genesis 1 in Mesopotamian culture, for example:

- the Atrahasis Epic, seventeenth century B.C.E.

- the Enuma Elish, twelfth century B.C.E.

- the Gilgamesh Epic, seventeenth century B.C.E.

The genres of history and myth are very different from one another. Written history can be wrong: the author intends to describe something correctly and then fails to do so. Symbolic stories, on the other hand, can be evaluated as good or bad, but they cannot be wrong. The author of the Genesis story is not writing history, nor is he addressing the question, "What happened?"

In the world of the ancient Israelites, the symbolic story was "real" yet different from the stories of Israel that begin with the introduction of Abraham and Sarah. Modern conservative Christians deny that any distinction needs to be made. Part of the problem is the dominance of Genesis 3, the story of Adam and Eve's sin, in Christian theology. In the interpretation of their sin as inherited in the Christian doctrine of original sin, Genesis 3 became an intrinsic component in the Christian understanding of the purpose of redemption and the function of Christ.

Modern history, like modern empirical science, has methods that guide inquiry and criteria by which to evaluate evidence for judgment. An Italian, Giovanni Battista Vico (d.

1744), is credited with laying the foundation for modern historical research, and Vico himself called it "the New Science." Historical questions have always been asked about the Bible, but the question, "Did this really happen?" defines modern interests in a way that had never been done before. The danger is that the historical question sometimes threatens to become the only question asked and to become the sole criterion for truth. The affirmation, "This is true," for many people has a single meaning: "Yes, this happened."

Purpose and Context

Preoccupation with cultic and ritual matters in the larger narrative of the Torah suggests that the author is closely associated with the Jerusalem temple and its sacrifices and liturgies. During the period of the Babylonian exile of (primarily) the elites of Judah, a group of priests, drawing on ancient traditions, wrote down their traditions as a way of preserving them in a time of extreme uncertainty. In the Documentary Hypothesis, the composition theory of the Torah, scholars designate this group as singular, the priestly writers, and by the letter P.[3]

---

3. Julius Wellhausen (d. 1918) introduced the theory in his work on the prolegomenon to the history of Israel in 1883. Building on insights from writers as far back as the Middle Ages, Wellhausen argued persuasively that there is more than one tradition ("writer") underlying the initial composition of the Torah. His theory is influential especially for establishing a framework for identifying these sources and dating them. A brief account of the theory is given in Kee et al., *The Cambridge Companion to the Bible*, 36–42. Clues that the unified narrative as we have it was based on different earlier traditions are, for example, the use of different names for divine reality, the disparity between customs that date to a certain time and their appearance in stories of a much

The author's purpose in the first Genesis creation story was meta-historical rather than historical and personal rather than theoretical. He is not recording a revelation of *how* things came to be. The *how* is a particularly modern preoccupation. P's concern is proclaiming the goodness of both the universe and its transcendent source. He grounds the universe and its value in the freedom of divine choice to bring it into existence. Why he does so is intimately linked with the historical situation.

Scholars date the first Genesis story to the sixth century B.C.E. The Babylonians had been victorious over Judah and, after the conquest, took the defeated people of Judah back to Babylon. The Babylonians destroyed the city of Jerusalem and Solomon's temple. The conquest was a catastrophic event for the people of Judah. Those left behind were in bondage to foreign rulers in their own land. Those taken captive were in bondage to their oppressors in a foreign land. The priestly writers' context is one of suffering and despair.

In face of this catastrophe, P clearly affirms God's uniqueness and power. Because God is good, the universe that God brings into being is good as well. Lest the hearer miss this point, it is repeated through the narrative as a refrain. Even in the face of the radical evil of destruction and exile, the author proclaims that God and creation are good. The author affirms Israel's God, Yahweh, as the ultimate and only divine power over the universe. There is no divine consort (as in competing creation stories in the culture). There is no divine dualism, i.e., a divine principle of good and one of evil.

----

earlier period, and conflicting perspectives on issues such as kingship. See ibid., 43–51, for a more extended discussion of myth in the ancient world.

It is not hard to see why creation has been imagined as the divine activity of making things. "Creation" for fundamentalist creationists refers to Genesis 1. Specifically, it is the idea of "special creation." God creates each particular thing as it is. When creation carries this meaning, evolution is pitted against it as an opposing way of accounting for *things*. In the picture language of poetry, God is "up there" making things for "down here." The reality that is beyond image is expressed in "picture language" by the poet. God acts. God creates things. But to take the picture language literally as "what happened," as history, misunderstands poetry and symbolic narrative. What the biblical writer expresses by "up" is transcendence. God is in some sense beyond the world, distinct from the world. As long as one remains in the world of common sense, transcendence and contingency are conveyed through dramatic images and symbols and narrative. To understand what the biblical writer affirms symbolically—transcendent power, contingency, creation—we have to move out of picture language and into the realm of systematic meaning. Terms are defined and relations articulated.

In Genesis 1 human beings are created together as the apex of God's creative activity. Their origin is portrayed differently in the creation story that follows in Genesis 2. The author of this second narrative is referred to as J, for the Jahwist writer (as Yahwist was spelled in German). It is dated around the tenth century B.C.E. and is thought to originate in the context of Solomon's court. In J's story only one human is created at first. This human is an "earthling," a genderless creature, *ha-ʾadam* in Hebrew.[4] God takes dust from the earth and breathes into it to make the earth creature.

4. For an analysis of Genesis 2–3, see Trible, "A Love Story Gone Awry."

Both Genesis 1 and Genesis 2 contain commands. The command in Genesis 1 is positive: "Be fruitful and multiply." To fulfill this requirement requires the intimacy of sexual relationships and the social world of marriage. The command in Genesis 2 is negative. The *ha-ʾadam* is not to eat from one of the trees in the garden, the tree of knowledge of good and evil. One can see what is coming.

Then begins a search for a companion for the *ha-ʾadam*. Creatures are brought to the *ha-ʾadam*, but none are suitable as a companion. Finally, God waits for the *ha-ʾadam* to sleep and, taking a rib from its genderless body, forms a second creature. With two humans, J introduces the gendered Hebrew words for male and female, *ʾiš* and *ʾiššah*, male and female. Man was not created first and woman second. Created first was the *ha-ʾadam*, then the two distinct beings, *ʾiš* and *ʾiššah*. The command to the earthling becomes a command for the two of them. Disobedience is a separate story.

The first creation story stands on its own. It is a poetic masterpiece that is complete from its first to last lines. But the second creation story is obviously part one of a two-part story. The first character in J's second story is a talking serpent who asks the woman about the command. She knows and repeats it. The snake then gives his reading of the divine command: "For God knows that in that day you eat of it your eyes will be opened, and you will be like God, knowing good and evil" (3:5).

In literary terms, "knowing good and evil" is a *merism*, a totality. Knowledge of good and evil is knowledge of the whole. Genuine knowledge of the whole is wisdom. To know good and evil is itself a good, at least in the absence of a command prohibiting the fruit that would give it. The woman wants what the snake is tempting her with. She takes from the forbidden tree and eats and gives some to her husband. He too eats. Violation of the command brings estrangement between God and the humans.

The couple hides from God in shame in the garden. When found, they are each given a punishment and sent out from the garden. Theirs is just the first sin. More will come. This one sets the stage for the story of the family of Abraham and Sarah, God's redemptive solution to the problem of sin.

The stories in Genesis 1–3 are symbolic narratives. The authors do not have modern concerns in mind. The primary question for people today about the universe is: "How did it happen?" Even though we find descriptions and images of an original creative event in the Scriptures, they are not a response to this kind of question of origin. Their question was much more one of "Who is God for us?" That God is creator of all that exists is a monotheistic affirmation made in the midst of a time of great despair.

BIBLICAL CREATION FAITH

The Hebrew Bible is replete with creation texts calling forth praise and thanksgiving for God's wisdom and creative activity. Genesis 1 and 2 are just the first of many passages expressing the creation faith of the people of ancient Israel and Judah. Several examples are given below.

Psalms

The Psalms frequently refer to creation. In Ps 121:2 the psalmist asks from where help will come, defining divine reality as

Creator in his answer: "My help comes from the LORD, who made heaven and earth." Psalm 24 emphasizes—perhaps over against the view of the elite that it is theirs—that the earth belongs to God because God has brought it into existence: "The earth is the LORD's, and all its fullness, the world and those who dwell within. For he has founded it upon the seas, and established it upon the waters" (24:1–2). In Psalm 8, the heavens are "the work of your hands" (8:3). Psalm 104 is very much like Genesis 1 in its praise of God as Creator. In order to emphasize that all things have their ultimate origin in God, it names things in our experience, as did Genesis 1. Its celebration of God's greatness extends beyond things in the realm of nature to the domestic realm of table fellowship and bread, oil, and wine:

> O LORD my God, you are very great.
> You are clothed with honor and majesty,
>> wrapped in light as with a garment.
> You stretch out the heavens like a tent . . .
> You set the earth on its foundations
>> that it shall never be shaken . . .
> You cause springs to gush forth in the valleys . . .
>
> You cause the grass to grow for the cattle,
>> and plants for people to use,
> to bring forth food from the earth
>> and wine to gladden the human heart,
> oil to make the face shine,
>> and bread to strengthen the human heart.
> (Ps 104:1–2, 5, 10, 14–15)

Psalm 95 again defines the God of Israel as Creator, giving in abbreviated form the highlights of a universe brought about by divine choice:

> For the LORD is a great God,
>> and a great King above all gods.
> In his hand are the depths of the earth;
>> the heights of the mountain are his also.
> The sea is his, for he made it,
>> and the dry land, which his hands have formed.
> (Ps 95:3–5)

Israel's relationship to God is rooted in God's creative activity. God not only creates stars and mountains but the people of Israel as well:

> Know that the LORD is God.
>> It is he that made us, and we are his . . .
> For the LORD is good,
>> his steadfast love endures forever,
>> and his faithfulness to all generations.
> (Ps 100:3, 5)

The response of human beings to God's creative activity is ethical:

> The earth is the LORD's and all that is in it,
>> the world, and those who live in it . . .
> Who shall ascend the hill of the LORD?
>> And who shall stand in his holy place?
> Those who have clean hands and pure hearts,
>> who do not lift up their souls to what is false,
>> and do not swear deceitfully. (Ps 24:1, 3)

Creation is distorted by evil, thus the recurring themes of suffering and evil as well as justice. "The LORD loves those who hate evil," and separates the righteous from the wicked (Ps 97:10). God is the "lover of justice," the one who establishes and executes justice (Ps 99:4).

Wisdom Literature

The Wisdom literature makes a unique contribution to biblical creation faith. God's creative wisdom is personified as a woman. What is gender-neutral in English, wisdom, is striking in Greek as a feminine noun, *Sophia*. Wisdom in Hebrew is a feminine noun, too, *ḥokmah*.

The Sophia image is one believing community's apprehension of divine reality. She is not a rival God but a personification of God's reason. Creative and compassionate, Sophia has all of God's attributes. In Proverbs, Sophia's description of her existence prior to creation is itself a creation story:

> The LORD created me at the beginning of his work,
> > the first of his acts of long ago.
> Ages ago I was set up, at the first,
> > before the beginning of the earth.
> When there were no depths I was brought forth,
> > when there were no springs abounding with water.
> Before the mountains had been shaped,
> > before the hills, I was brought forth
> when he had not yet made earth and fields,
> > or the world's first bits of soil.
> When he established the heavens, I was there,
> > when he drew a circle on the face of the deep,

> when he made firm the skies above,
>> when he established the fountains of the deep,
> when he assigned to the sea its limit,
>> so that the waters might not transgress his command,
> when he marked out the foundations of the earth,
>> then I was beside him, like a master worker,
> and I was daily his delight,
>> rejoicing before him always,
> rejoicing in his inhabited world
>> and delighting in the human race. (Prov 8:22–31)

Sophia's value is not abstract but concrete. She is the difference between life and death:

> For whoever finds me finds life
>> and obtains favor from the LORD;
> but those who miss me injure themselves;
>> all who hate me love death. (Prov 8:35–36)

Also wisdom literature, the book of Job is the story of one catastrophe after another falling on a faithful and righteous man, Job, all to test the genuineness of his faith. Here the creation story comes from God's voice as a response to Job's questioning of his misfortune and suffering:

> Where were you when I laid the foundation of the earth?
>> Tell me, if you have understanding.
> Who determined its measurements—surely you know!
>> Or who stretched the line upon it?
> On what were its bases sunk,
>> or who laid its cornerstone,

when the morning stars sang together
>   and all the heavenly beings shouted for joy?
> Or who shut in the sea with doors
>   when it burst out from the womb?
> —when I made the clouds its garment,
>   and thick darkness its swaddling band,
> and prescribed bounds for it,
>   and set bars and doors,
> and said, "Thus far shall you come, and no farther,
>   and here shall your proud waves be stopped"?
> (Job 38:4–11)

Sirach and the Wisdom of Solomon are noncanonical works, what Protestants call *apocryphal* and Catholics *deuterocanonical*. Sophia appears in both of these texts. Sirach starts with a testimony to Sophia:

> Sophia was created before all other things
>   and prudent understanding from eternity.
> The root of wisdom—to whom has it been revealed?
>   Her subtleties—who knows them?
> There is but one who is wise, greatly to be feared,
>   seated upon his throne—the Lord.
> It was he who created her;
>   he saw her and took her measure;
>   he poured her out upon his works,
> upon all the living according to his gift;
>   he lavished her upon those who love him.
> (Sir 1:4–10)

In describing divine creative activity, Sirach emphasizes order:

> When the Lord created his works from the beginning
>> and, in making them, determined their boundaries,
> he arranged his works in an eternal order,
>> and their dominion for all generations . . .
> Then the Lord looked upon the earth
>> and filled it with his good things.
> With all kinds of living beings he covered its surface,
>> and into it they must return. (Sir 16:26–27, 29–30)

Humans are part of these living things: "The Lord created human beings out of the earth, and makes them return to it again" (17:1). They are given authority over everything on earth. Filled with knowledge, they are made in God's image with minds for thinking (3–6). Unlike Genesis 2, here God shows humans good and evil (7). The covenant relation between God and humans is part of creation, as is the instruction, "Beware of all evil" and a commandment, whose specific content is taken for granted, "to each of them concerning the neighbor" (14).

The Wisdom of Solomon has much to say about Sophia. The reader is instructed to honor wisdom, so that you may reign forever.

> I will tell you what wisdom is and how she came to be,
>> and I will hide no secrets from you,
> but I will trace her course from the beginning of creation,
>> and make knowledge of her clear . . . (Wis 6:21–22)

She is:

> a breath of the power of God,
>> and a pure emanation of the glory of the Almighty;
>> therefore nothing defiled gains entrance into her.
> For she is a reflection of eternal light,
>> a spotless mirror of the working of God,
>> and an image of his goodness.
> Although she is but one,
>> she can do all things,
> and while remaining in herself,
>> she renews all things,
> in every generation she passes into holy souls
>> and makes them friends of God, and prophets,
> for God loves nothing so much as the person who lives with wisdom. (Wis 7:25–28)

We find the Sophia image in the New Testament, too. Jesus identified himself as Sophia's prophet.[5] It is a christological image for both Paul and the Synoptic Gospels—Matthew, Mark, and Luke. John's Gospel shifts from *Sophia* to *Logos*. The two terms "wisdom" and "reason" are functionally equivalent. The writer may have thought that it was more coherent to use the masculine *Logos* with the historical Jesus rather than the feminine *Sophia*. The Prologue of John's Gospel is a hymn and an incarnational creation story. Like Genesis 1, its emphasis is on the Word of creation. The divine Word is identified with Christ, who comes into the world as God's representative.

5. See, for example, Schüssler Fiorenza, *Jesus: Miriam's Child, Sophia's Prophet*. Or more generally as a prophetic figure and messenger of wisdom, see Theissen and Merz, *The Historical Jesus*, 95; the authors refer to the proclamation of Jesus as "incarnate wisdom," 123.

In the beginning was the Word,

    and the Word was with God,

    and the Word was God.

He was in the beginning with God.

All things came into being through him,

    and without him not one thing came into being . . .

He was in the world,

    and the world came into being through him;

    yet the world did not know him . . .

And the Word became flesh and lived among us,

    and we have seen his glory,

the glory as of a father's only son,

    full of grace and truth. (John 1:1–3, 10, 14)

INTERPRETATION

We started with the observation that the Bible is a complex work. It is interpreted correctly with the help of those who know its original languages, historical settings, cultural influences, literary structures, and theological themes.

Modern conservatives who insist on interpreting texts literally actually do the texts a great injustice by making them answer questions that are not their own. To pose Genesis 1 as an alternative to evolutionary theory misses its original purpose and meaning, to say nothing of totally misrepresenting its literary genre. To make creation into a historical event misses the transcendent meaning of creation that the author intended to convey. Those who claim that the literalist interpretation was the original approach of the church do not know the actual history of the church. Historical evidence does not support their claim. To name only one prominent figure, in Irenaeus's book, *Against Celsus,* the third-century theologian opposed the view of those who took the time of six days for creation literally (96:6).

Genesis 1 and evolutionary theory are completely different. They should not be compared, nor do they represent two alternatives from which we must chose. Evolutionary theory is a technical account of the development of diversity and complexity in the physical world based on the evidence gathered in scientific research. Genesis 1 is a poetic and symbolic narrative, devoted to praise of God as Creator, written to encourage those in despair over the loss of their land, their temple, and their freedom. They are not choices but two very different apprehensions of reality. To make either answer the question of the other is to miss their function and insight.

Biblical creation faith is, at root, praise and thanksgiving. We see this clearly in the Psalms: "My mouth will speak the praise of the LORD, and all flesh will bless his holy name forever and ever" (Ps 145:21). Even the heavens are called to praise in yet another creation text:

> Praise the LORD!
> Praise the LORD from the heavens;
>> praise him in the heights!
> Praise him, all his angels;
>> praise him, all his host!
> Praise him, sun and moon;
>> praise him, all you shining stars!
> Praise him, you highest heavens,
>> and you waters above the heavens!

> Let them praise the name of the LORD,
>> for he commanded and they were created . . .
> Praise the LORD from the earth . . .
> Kings of the earth and all peoples . . .
> Let them praise the name of the LORD,
>> for his name alone is exalted;
>> his glory is above earth and heaven.

(Ps 148:1–5, 7, 11, 13)

TWO

The Meaning of Creation

Christian faith arose as proclamation. It spread through itinerate preaching and an ever-expanding establishment of religious assemblies, associated with Jewish synagogues. But what was easily proclaimed in the first generation later became the subject of scrutiny as new questions arose. The core proclamation of the Jesus movement was that God had validated the message and person of Jesus by raising him from the dead. It yielded a centuries-long inquiry into the relation of the Son—the risen Christ—to the Father. The many ways in which this relation could be understood are evident in the number of what today are called heresies but were, at the time, possible ways of apprehending this relation. This process of finding the appropriate terms and relations for conceiving divine nature was the way of doctrinal development. *Doctrine* means authoritative teaching. Doctrine results from a definitive settling of questions. It sets the boundaries for what is to be believed, beyond which lies the unacceptable and inappropriate. For better or worse, doctrine eliminated the ambiguity inherent in proclamation to authorize a particular expression as the right way of talking about a particular dimension of faith, here, the relation of Son and Father in divine nature. Similarly, the doctrine of creation emerged from the early

Christian and Jewish affirmation of divine reality as Creator. Creeds affirm these components of faith.

But in addition to the development of individual doctrines, the concept of doctrine itself has evolved. In the earliest stages of Christianity doctrine referred to instruction. In the New Testament, doctrine and catechesis are synonymous. Women and men drawn by the Jesus followers' preaching of the risen Christ underwent a process of initiation. Doctrine and catechesis denoted both the act of instructing and the content of the instruction in this process. As questions arose about faith and theologians dealt more systematically with numerous topics, the use of the term *doctrine* shifted from catechesis to these theological conclusions. So Augustine's exploration of sin is referred to as his "doctrine of sin."

In turn, these theological studies constituted the primary resource from which church councils drew when the need arose to formulate the boundaries of faith. But by the medieval period, the meaning of doctrine had again shifted. It no longer referred to an individual theologian's study of a particular topic but to the conciliar formulation of belief itself. What was to be believed about God as Creator is found not only in the doctrine of creation but is also embedded in the christological and trinitarian doctrines as well as the doctrine of original sin.

The major features of the Christian understanding of creation were in place by the time of Augustine, Bishop of Hippo, in the fifth century. A prolific writer, Augustine wrote several works on creation. He saw the danger in misinterpreting the scriptures for the lessened respect a Christian would receive from a non-Christian. Christians should not make fools of themselves by reading the Bible inappropriately:

It is too disgraceful and ruinous, though, and
greatly to be avoided, that [the non-Christian]
should hear a Christian speaking so idiotically on
these matters, and as if in accord with Christian
writings, that he might say that he could scarcely
keep from laughing when he saw how totally in
error they are. In view of this and in keeping it in
mind constantly while dealing with the book of
Genesis, I have, insofar as I was able, explained in
detail and set forth for consideration the meanings
of obscure passages, taking care not to affirm rashly
some one meaning to the prejudice of another and
perhaps better explanation.[1]

Creatio ex nihilo, the centerpiece of the Christian theology of creation, was generally accepted by Augustine's time;
but it had not yet been integrated into creeds. The Fourth
Lateran Council in 1215 C.E. included it in its first canon on
Christian belief, the treatise on God:

We firmly believe and openly confess that there is
only one true God, eternal and immense, omnipotent, unchangeable, incomprehensible, and inef-
fable, Father, Son, and Holy Ghost; three Persons
indeed but one essence, substance, or nature abso-
lutely simple; the Father (proceeding) from no one,
but the Son from the Father only, and the Holy
Ghost equally from both, always without beginning and end. The Father begetting, the Son begot-
ten, and the Holy Ghost proceeding; consubstantial
and coequal, co-omnipotent and coeternal, the
one principle of the universe, Creator of all things
invisible and visible, spiritual and corporeal, who

1. Augustine, "The Literal Interpretation of Genesis," on 1:19–20.

from the beginning of time and by His omnipotent
power *made from nothing* creatures both spiritual
and corporeal, angelic, namely, and mundane, and
then human, as it were, common, composed of
spirit and body.[2]

Six centuries later, in its second session in 1870, the
First Vatican Council reaffirmed *creatio ex nihilo*. The cultural horizon of this council was very different from that of
the medieval Lateran Council.[3] Vatican I was the first church
council to meet after the publication of Charles Darwin's *The
Origin of Species* in 1859.

Without question, the world of those at Vatican I had
changed from the medieval world assumed by the church for
so long. In the static world of the medievals, stability and order were highly valued—the more the world stayed the same,
the better it was. God's unchanging nature was a sign of God's
perfection.

This static world disappeared with the discoveries that
affirmed the evolutionary character of the universe. The universe is dynamic, not static. It is instructive, given this total
transformation of image, that the way the conciliar writers
defined God fit either world. God is the source of all that is.
The universe is the product of a freely-willed decision originating in divine goodness. The council affirmed the traditional distinction between reason and faith, reinforcing the

2. Medieval Sourcebook. Twelfth Ecumenical Council, 1215. Italics
added. Online: http://www.fordham.edu/halsall/basis/lateran4.html.

3. First Vatican Council, 1869–70. Second Session, 1870. Dogmatic
Constitution on the Church. Chapter 1 and Canon 1, "On God the Creator of All Things." Chapter 4, Canon 4, "On Reason and Faith." Online:
http://www.ewtn.com/library/COUNCILS/V1.html.

integrity of each as a distinct way of knowing. Science was included in what they meant by reason.

The hurdle that Vatican I set for the acceptance of scientific conclusions, however, was high. To be true, scientific conclusions must conform to church doctrines. Of particular concern here was the doctrine of original sin. New insights about the earth's past and human history from various scientific fields bore specific implications for this doctrine. The question of the historicity of Adam and Eve was of paramount importance.

Because the doctrine of original sin came to have so much influence on the way in which the purpose of Christ has been understood, Genesis 3 and original sin have been subjects of intense debate in the modern period. In the end, Vatican I expressed caution about these new insights about the past that accompanied evolutionary theory. But they did not reject the theory outright as they did some views of the world and God, such as pantheism and materialism.

In 1950, Pope Pius XII's encyclical, *Humani generis,* addressed evolutionary theory along with other modern ideas that threatened, in his view, to undermine the foundations of Catholic doctrine. The pope instructed theologians that they were to teach the official teachings of the church and not just their personal opinions.

Evolution was introduced by the assertion that there was no sufficient basis for a comprehensive belief in evolution. Yet Catholics were to consider the origin of the body of human beings a legitimate subject.

A decade later the Second Vatican Council (1962–65) addressed the question of *why* God creates, shifting from the traditional language of divine willing and the good to the relational and personal language of love: "Creation comes about 'out of love' (*ex amore*), out of God's creative love . . ." (*Gaudium et Spes*, #2). This way of thinking of creation draws on the theological concept of *kenosis,* the idea that God's "self-emptying" brings finite being into existence. *Kenosis* is rooted in the conception of God's nature as relational.

Gaudium et Spes, "The Church in the Modern World," one of Vatican II's more important documents, specifically addressed the transition in scientific understanding from a static to a dynamic worldview. It affirmed the independence of scientific inquiry, indeed, the independence of the universe: "For by the very circumstance of their having been created, all things are endowed with their own stability, truth, goodness, proper laws and order" (#36).

Such an affirmation of independence, however, does not mean that creatures are independent of God. As intrinsically contingent, they are dependent on an ultimate source for their existence. "For without the Creator, the creature would disappear" (#36). Grounding scientific insights and discoveries in God, who "holds all things in existence," the conciliar writers reject the position that science and religion are opposed, "for earthly matters and the concerns of faith derive from the same God" (#36). They go further to criticize those Christians who do not "sufficiently attend to the rightful independence of science" (#36). They are responsible for the misunderstanding that faith and science are opposed. Significant by its absence in the document is the condition of conformity with church doctrine that Vatican I imposed on scientific truth.

The Christian theological and conciliar tradition developed the themes of biblical creation faith. Judgments made about creation are judgments about God. For God to be truly

God, matter cannot be eternal. In its entirety, time as well as matter, the universe is contingent. Only its source is eternal and without cause. For God to be truly *God*, finite being cannot be necessary. If God necessarily wills the world, then the world is necessary to God and God is dependent on the world. God does not create out of necessity but freely. For God to be God, the radical dependence of finite being on God must be permanent. God is not responsible just for the origin of the universe, a past event. The universe is always dependent on God for its existence.

THEOLOGICAL SPECULATION

Theological debate in the first centuries of the church was energized by defense of the Christian proclamation of salvation. This proclamation was at once christological (about the person and work of Jesus) and anthropological (about what it means to be human in this light). On the christological side, Christians asserted that, through Christ, God offered salvation to all humankind and that Christ's redemption from sin mediated reconciliation with God. What humankind needs, Christ offers. This implied an anthropological judgment. If reconciliation was necessary for all people, then sinfulness must be universal.

To ground this twofold claim, Christian theologians looked at the story of Adam and Eve with different eyes than had their Israelite and Judean predecessors.[4] For the Israelites, Genesis 3 was important as the story of the first sin, but it played little role outside its own context. The story did not have particular significance in Jewish theology. But Christian

4. See Wiley, *Original Sin*, 13–36, 56–75.

theologians looked to it with their own question of the universality of sin. How did we get from the *first* sin to *universal* sinfulness? Christ's redemption was necessary only if all were in need of it.

Like Darwin centuries later in his search for the mechanism of evolution, theologians sought the mechanism, so to speak, of universal sinfulness. For some theologians, the principle was ontological: all humankind was somehow *in* Adam. When Adam sinned, all sinned. With Augustine of Hippo, this image gradually gave way to a principle of biological inheritance: humanity is sinful because all have *inherited* Adam's sin. While a few voices expressed reservations about this explanation, no one protested strongly that this mixture of biological and moral categories was problematic in itself.

This is the meaning of *original sin* in the Christian theological tradition. The first sin is that of Adam and Eve. *Original* does not mean "first" but "inherited." Original sin is the inheritance of this first sin through procreation. In the fifth century, Augustine of Hippo took this idea from the tradition as the centerpiece of his reflections on sin and grace. He gave it the finishing touch.

Once the doctrine of original sin was in place, all other theological categories revolved around it. Original sin became the reason for the Incarnation itself. The catechetical question and response are familiar: "Why did Christ come? To save us from original sin." This was not the only way the Incarnation and redemption were understood or could be understood, but this became the dominant interpretation. Fundamentalists today understand Christ exclusively in this way.

But the first Christian centuries required more of theologians than finding the explanatory principle for the universal sinfulness of humanity. The Mediterranean world in which Christianity took root was replete with religious and philosophical views about the origin of the world. The question, "Why is there something rather than nothing?" received many answers. We will look at three: the approach generally designated as Gnosticism and the views of the Greek philosophers Plato and Aristotle. Each view challenged Christian thinkers to refine and clarify their theological convictions about creation.

Gnosticism

The term *Gnosticism* comes from the Greek word for knowledge, *gnōsis*. Gnostic groups were characterized by belief in a secret revelation.[5] The enlightenment they received through revelation was the means of freeing them from bondage to the inferior world of matter and enabling their return to the nonmaterial divine source of their existence. Gnostic systems are dualist. They conceive of the divine as two transcendent deities, one the principle of good, the other the principle of evil.

One of the first Christians to challenge Gnostic views was the second-century Bishop of Lyons, Irenaeus (d. ca. 202 C.E.). In his *Adversus haereses* (Against Heresies), he was concerned in particular with the followers of the Gnostic teacher Valentinus; but the book as a whole is a refutation of Gnosticism. Against the Gnostics' dualist conception of the divine as an utterly transcendent "High God" and an inferior "Demiurge" or Creator, Irenaeus stressed the unity of God.

5. On Gnosticism, see Perkins, *The Gnostic Dialogue*; idem, *Gnosticism in the New Testament*; and Pearson, *Ancient Gnosticism*.

There is one God who is Creator of everything that is. From the biblical doctrine of God, expressed in Genesis 1 and other texts, Irenaeus emphasized God's transcendent otherness and immense power. God does not create from preexisting matter but *speaks* the universe into existence. There is no inferiority in the act of creating.

Against the Gnostic view that creation is the work of a lesser god and that material reality is evil—thus the body embedded in matter is evil—Irenaeus stressed the goodness of matter. Creation is a divine choice and an expression of transcendent freedom. Irenaeus brought creation and christology together by arguing that creation was oriented from the start toward Christ and redemption. Despite the distortion caused by sin, history moves the world toward its consummation in Christ. From the apostle Paul, Irenaeus took the idea of the "recapitulation of all things in Christ." In the Incarnation the Word of God assumes human nature in its entirety. Christ is the new Adam who unifies and leads humankind back to God. Through Christ, all things are restored.

Irenaeus stressed the Incarnation over against Christian Gnostics who separated the creator God of the Hebrew Bible from the God of the New Testament, naming the former evil and the latter good. Stressing the oneness of God, Irenaeus emphasized that the Father of Jesus Christ alone is God. In Jesus Christ *God* had become human. In becoming part of the natural world, God blessed and redeemed creation. The body of Jesus was not evil but the sacramental bearer of the divine. In the redemptive event of the Incarnation Irenaeus saw the divinization of humankind: "The Word became flesh and the Son of God became the Son of man, so that man, by entering into communion with the Word, and thus receiving divine sonship, might become a son of God" (*Adv. haer.* 3.19.1).

Athanasius (d. 373 C.E.), the fourth-century Bishop of Alexandria, took up this theme of divinization, saying of Christ: "He, indeed, assumed humanity that we might become God." Divinization became a theological principle: the incarnational dimension of God's presence in the world emphasized by Christian theologians reinforced both divine immanence and transcendence. God is radically transcendent, other than the universe, but also radically immanent, present to the universe. This view of God as "in" the universe but "more than" the universe is called *panentheism*. (It is not to be confused with pantheism, the identification of God with the universe.) In Jesus, God is radically *natural*.

Greek Philosophers

Along with Gnostic views, Christian theologians countered the prevailing philosophical view that matter was eternal. The primary Greek concept was not creation but eternity. Plato assumed that matter and form, the two elements of nature, were eternal; the cosmos had always existed. The divine reality who creates in the *Timaeus*, Plato's late Socratic dialogue, is a Demiurge, like an artisan or craftsman rather than the transcendent reality Christians would later affirm. The Demiurge shapes and fashions the material world from pre-existing chaotic matter. While divine, the Demiurge is not an omnipotent power over nature, nor is the universe utterly dependent on it for its existence.

Aristotle, too, argued that matter was eternal. In his *Physics*, Aristotle addressed creation in the context of a theory of change. Things in the universe are undergoing change all the time. They are always in a state of potentiality—existing as what they are but potentially something else, what they are to become. They change by the principle of motion. Motion is the fulfillment of what exists potentially.

To change from potentiality to actuality, an efficient cause—a *mover*—is required. Yet, unless the *unmoved mover*—without cause—is *one*, there would be an infinite regress of efficient causes or movers. The unmoved mover is pure actuality with no potentiality. The unmoved mover set the universe into motion: thus the eternity of matter. Time, the measure of motion, is eternal as well. The logical necessity of an unmoved mover is Aristotle's argument in Book 8 of the *Physics*. Without such a cause, he held, one could not explain other motion. The universe needs the unmoved mover to remain in existence.

While Aristotle's unmoved mover is the first cause, as is the Christian conception of God, because of the eternity of matter the unmoved mover is not fully transcendent over the universe. The universe does not have the kind of radical dependence on it that the Christian concept of *creatio ex nihilo* (creation out of nothing) will assert. For Christians, there is *nothing* except God until God brings the universe into existence. Augustine will emphasize that even time is created. What the Genesis narrator separates into six days is not separated in the divine act. God creates everything simultaneously (*Confessions*, Book 11).

Other philosophical groups, such as the Stoics and Epicureans, also presumed the eternity of matter. This shared judgment originated in a practical observation: something comes from something or, to put it negatively, nothing can come from nothing. To meet these cultural challenges, Christian theologians had to go beyond the praise of God's transcendence in biblical creation faith to introduce technical terms and systematic meaning. "Nothing can come from nothing," unless the one creating is creating existence itself. This is the principle of *creatio ex nihilo.* What is clear from an overview of comments of Christian theologians from the first centuries of the church is that they did not defend a literal interpretation of Genesis 1, nor did they use the text of Genesis 1 to counter other views. They assume the perspective of Genesis 1—the unity and transcendence of God, the goodness of creation—but they were not bound by the text of Genesis 1 in any way, certainly not in any literalist way.

The emerging doctrine of creation in the early church was at once a doctrine of God, too. The earliest references to the principle of *creatio ex nihilo* are in the work of a noncanonical work called the *Shepherd of Hermas*, thought to be early second-century; see the earlier parallels in 2 Macc 7:28; Rom 4:17; and Heb 11:3. The principle is mentioned first in a vision Hermas has of a woman speaking to him from heaven who refers to "God, who dwells in the heavens, and made out of nothing the things that exist" (1:1). The second reference is in discussion about the first commandment, on faith in God. Hermas writes: "Believe first of all that there is one God who created and finished all things, and made all things out of nothing. He alone is able to contain the whole, but Himself cannot be contained" (2:1).

Irenaeus, the second-century Bishop of Lyons, noted above for his response to the Gnostics, also emphasized the link between creation and existence: "Men, indeed, are not able to make something from nothing, but only from existing material. God, however, is greater than men first of all in this: that when nothing existed beforehand, he called into existence the very material for his creation" (*Adv. Haer.* 2.10.4).

By the third century, the ideas of the unity of God and *creatio ex nihilo* were "the rule of faith." Tertullian writes: "There is, however, a rule of faith; and so that we may acknowledge at this point what it is we defend, it is this precisely that we believe: There is only one God and none other besides him, the creator of the world who brought forth all things out of nothing through his Word, first of all sent forth" ("The Demurrer against the Heretics" 13:1).

Or again:

> He is the unique God for this reason alone, that he is the sole God, and he is the sole God for this reason alone, that nothing existed along with him. So too he must be the first, because all else is after him. All else is after him because all else is from him and from him because they are created out of nothing. The account of Scripture, then, is correct: "Who has known the mind of the Lord? Or who has been his counselor? Or whom has he consulted? Or who showed him the way of wisdom and knowledge? Who gave, and recompense will be made to him?"[6]

Augustine's methodological principle, *crede ut intelligas,* "Believe in order that you may understand," became a theological mantra of the tradition.[7] In his view, *trust in a reliable source* (faith) is an essential condition of understand-

6. Tertullian *Against Ermogenes* 17:1 (203 C.E.), and quoting Rom 11:33–36.

7. Augustine *Sermon* 43.7.9.

ing. Because God is the author of truth, faith and reason are complementary. Augustine's "divine illumination epistemology" brings God into relation with science, not as an alternative explanation to what scientists propose about the world but at the root of their understanding of the world. God illumines the human mind, making the world and divine truths intelligible. All knowledge is from God. In knowing what is, human beings come to know what God already knows.

While theologians in the early church rejected the eternity of the world as a prerequisite for affirming the total transcendence of God and the contingency of the universe, not all have thought that it was essential to reject it. Thomas Aquinas in the thirteenth century thought that even if the world was eternal it was still contingent. It is not self-existing, but dependent on God for its existence. This question remains a topic in contemporary theology and philosophy. Alfred North Whitehead, for example, the influential American process philosopher, conceived of God's nature as social and relational; in his view God and the world have always coexisted.

Systematic Meaning

In thinking about divine reality, the world, and the relation between them, Christian theologians started with biblical creation faith, gradually finding that the problems they addressed required ever more technical terms and distinctions to say precisely that they meant. While symbolic narratives such as Genesis 1 evoke powerful images and communicate meaning, they do not by themselves explain. Explanation requires the development of the capacity to think theoretically. Even while acknowledging that these matters remain mysteries, theology introduces a systematic realm of meaning in which distinctions and definitions capture an understanding of the subject "in itself" rather than in the common-sense mode of understanding it merely "in relation to me."[8]

In the development of the doctrine of creation, this move toward theory occurred gradually and in the work of many people. Two concepts are at the center of the theoretical apprehension of divine activity, *creatio ex nihilo* and *creatio continua*. The Christian doctrine of creation includes both.

The idea that God does not create from preexistent material is first a statement about God rather than about the universe. God's *transcendence* is God's complete independence from the world as well as the world's complete dependence on God for its existence.

By affirming that God creates from nothing, *creatio ex nihilo*, early Christian theologians moved beyond the common-sense principle that "something must come from something." We cannot *imagine* nothingness. We cannot *imagine* an uncaused cause and so on. But we can *think* about the world and God in such a way that cumulatively our conclusions become an interlocking set of judgments. If God creates from some pre-existing substance, for example, this substance is co-eternal with God. Then God is not independent of matter. If the universe is an extension of God's own substance, as in pantheism, God is part of nature. Here, too, God is not independent of matter. Both ways of thinking limit God's transcendence. If God is fully transcendent, matter is not eternal and God is independent of the world. *Creatio ex nihilo* expresses this judgment.

8. On theory and the theoretical differentiation of consciousness, see Lonergan, *Method in Theology*, for example, 81–82, 85, 304.

Similarly, we cannot *imagine* something finite having no cause. All finite things are dependent on another for their existence. But if God is not finite, God is not dependent on another for existence. God has no cause. The judgment that God is absolute (uncaused) comes from the rejection of contingency: If God is not *contingent*, God must be *uncaused*.

To affirm God as truly God, the classic Christian tradition usually reasoned, the eternity of matter and contingency of any sort in relation to God must be rejected. So, too, theologians rejected any necessity in God's creating. God gives existence to the created order not from any need or necessity but as a *free* act. By choice and decision, God brings the created order into being.

When creation is linked with Genesis 1, creation is imagined as in the past. It is also imagined as the creation of things. These images are unavoidable. Creation is "what happened." But in a theoretical apprehension of divine activity, creation is not an event in the past nor the creation of things as such but the *relation* of a contingent universe to its absolute source at every moment. God is at every moment sustaining the universe in its existence. *Creatio continua* (continuous creation) is the actualization of the universe.

Medieval Contribution

The response of Christian theologians to challenging viewpoints in the early church laid the foundation for the Christian doctrine of creation. They emphasized the contingency of the universe and God's freedom in bringing it into existence. They rejected dualist views, in which divine reality is twofold, one good and the other evil. They emphasized the full transcendence of God and power of nature. Judged less-than-fully transcendent were Plato's Demiurge and Aristotle's Prime Mover. The Christian theologians emphasized the difference between the world and God. God is not one with the world, as in pantheism, even if God is intimately present to it. Only God *is being*. Everything else *has being*.

Even in the early church, theologians were aware that significant thought was needed to bring scientific and theological views into relation with one another. Augustine, for example, was alert to potential conflicts, as we have seen, writing that Christians should not have dumb opinions about the natural world based on misreadings of the Bible, especially opinions that could be condemned as false by reason. The medieval theologian Thomas Aquinas, some eight centuries after Augustine, shared that sensitivity to the way in which Christians are regarded by others. He did not want Christians to be saying something from the perspective of faith that was known to be false from a scientific perspective.[9]

In his reflections on creation, Aquinas built further on the foundation of earlier theologians. He provided an explanatory precision to the meaning of creation. For him the question, "Why is there something rather than nothing?" reflects the natural desire to know. It is not beyond human beings to answer. Thomas knew Aristotle's *Physics*. But for Thomas, Aristotle's Prime Mover did not have what was most constitutive of God, the attribute of Creator. Aristotle's first cause is within the realm of natural causes. It is not the cause

9. Thomas Aquinas discusses creation in the *Summa Theologica*, Part I, qs. 44 and 45, online: http://wwww.newadvent.org/summa/104503.htm. A helpful introduction to Thomas and creation is Carroll, "Creation, Evolution, and Thomas Aquinas."

of existence itself. As Creator, God *gives* existence to the universe. Creation is the relation of dependence *in* creatures to an absolute source.

Creation is thus a cause but a unique cause, distinct from natural causes within the universe. To use a contemporary example, both religiously minded and scientifically minded persons refer to the Big Bang as "creation." The Big Bang is an event, a cosmic explosion generating the development of the universe. It is not the origin of existence but a natural cause. It may have been a singular cause, a once-in-a-universe change, but it was a *change*. Natural causes are changes in the universe. Creation is not a historical event like the Big Bang. Creation is a *relation* between finite and infinite reality. It accounts for being, not change.

While one should not equate the Big Bang and creation, neither should we separate them, as if we have to choose one or the other. Creation and natural causes are two different kinds of causality, both operative in the universe. What is probably of most significance in clarifying the way people talk about creation is eliminating the picture-thinking that imagines it as God's making things.

For Thomas, the fundamental meaning of God is as Creator. God's existence is demonstrated by the effects of God's work, namely, the universe itself. But, again, terminology may trip us up. To say that God "created the universe" invites images of God crafting *things*. But for Thomas it means, rather, that all things stand in a relationship of absolute dependence to a creator. This relation is not "out there" but in creatures. In other terms, existence is contingent. Created beings have being, while God is being. God gives existence to what was not. That a completely contingent universe exists is therefore due to God. It exists, too, with the full integrity of its own systems, laws, and causality. Things are the way they are because God has caused the whole universe to be governed by the laws intrinsic to it.

Scientists study changes and, in understanding them, identify natural causes. Their question is not *why* the universe exists—this they take for granted as the object of their inquiry—but *what* exists. This *what*, as we now know, is a dynamic world characterized by dramatic change. The knowledge of natural causes that scientists develop is different from the knowledge of the radical dependence of the universe on God as its ultimate source, as affirmed in the doctrine of creation. Evolution cannot be a threat to creation when they concern two very different aspects of reality; nor can it be a threat to God when God is the origin of the universe as it concretely exists.

Student Perceptions of Doctrine

It is one thing to say what a Christian doctrine is or what its development has been, and another to say what Christians themselves know of it. In the case of students, both Catholic and Protestant, in my own classes in a Catholic university, it is evident that even for those who come from families with deep ties to Christian communities and tradition, the understanding of doctrines is a bit tenuous. But their understanding of science is even more problematic, as is suggested below. The confusions are themselves interesting data for how this issue has been internalized. For this student, for example, science has a role in creating the universe. God is a little less than God:

> *God assisted in the beginning, when the universe was first developed. I think God had something to do with the molecules, the energy, that created the universe, along with science. Who is to say that God did not take the energy and use it to make the universe? I think God and science worked together. One required the assistance of the other in order to create what we know today as the universe.*

Here science is part of evolutionary reality:

> *The Big Bang theory explains to me the events that may have been set by God for science to play out.*

And for this person, science is a challenge to God, a situation giving rise to a dilemma:

> *If I were to side with the scientific approach to the story of Creation, I would feel like I was betraying God himself by allowing myself to believe that science is the only reputable answer to explaining our Creation.*

Some disparage scientific theory as "guess" or "opinion." Here the opposite has been done, giving theory a rather significant role:

> *I am intrigued with the notion that the universe was created by theories such as the Big Bang.*

Similarly, science is a competing creator:

> *How the universe was created is a controversy. Some say it was through scientific means and others say through the Bible and God.*

This student shifts science from a creating role to equivalence with evolution:

> *While religion says that God created the world, others believe that humans, animals, and all other life forms came about scientifically.*

The significance of science looms large for this student:

> *Science might be God's way of creating us.*

This student puts it even more boldly:

> *Is God or Science creator of the world?*

God has a role in filling in the gaps for this student:

> *There are points in the scientific argument that are unexplainable and things that must just be taken as given. This is where I believe God comes in, to explain the unexplainable.*

As these comments show, the work to be done in clarifying the controversy over creation and evolution is considerable. Rather than the study of the universe and its intelligible patterns, "science" is often understood to be the laws themselves. Our next chapter attempts to clarify evolution and the scientific quest of which it is a part.

THREE

Method, Truth, and Evolutionary Science

For over a century fundamentalist Christians in the United States have engaged in open resistance to Charles Darwin's theory of evolution. Their success in removing evolution from public school science programs or diminishing its value in the minds of students by disclaimers in books has invited lawsuits and resulted in censure of their agenda and goals. Christian conservatives have put great pressure on school boards across the nation to integrate the biblical story of creation into science courses treating the world's origins. Whole towns are divided because of their insistence on balancing evolution with their understanding of creation. Fundamentalists see "Darwinism" as more than a scientific theory about the natural world and its development. It presents to them the threat of an atheist and materialist view of the world. It undercuts the foundation for morality. It threatens the salvation of those who believe it rather than creationism.

Not everyone, of course, takes evolutionary theory as a threat to their eternal destiny. The scientific community shares a universal consensus that the evidence for evolution is "overwhelming." It is not feared but welcomed as a concept that makes sense of the data studied by a whole range of sciences. What is evolutionary theory and, in particular, Charles

Darwin's contribution to it? We will offset the opposition to Darwin, prefaced above and further probed in chapter 5, by examining the main lines of the theory of evolution in this chapter.

EVOLUTIONARY THINKING

By the reaction of religious conservatives, one would think that the idea of evolution was new. But evolutionary thinking is neither recent nor radical. By the time of Charles Darwin, scientists were quite familiar with the sequential order in which fossils appear in layers of rock: the lower the layer, the more primitive the fossil. The consistency of this fossil sequence was itself compelling evidence for evolution—not just development over time, but a change in species over time. The huge body of fossil evidence studied by geologists and paleontologists is foundational for what Darwin called *descent with modification*.

On the basis of fossil evidence and other means of verification, scientists extended the age of the planet further and further into the past. Fossil deposits reveal systematic changes over a nearly five-billion-year history of the Earth. Moreover, they point to a common ancestor from which all living things have descended. Molecular biology, a new scientific discipline emerging after Darwin's time, complemented fossil evidence with insights into genes and the role of genetic modification in evolution.[1]

1. The response of the scientific community to the threat posed to science programs by creationists has resulted in a wide range of informative articles, books, and website material. Helpful for this chapter in particular are: Ayala, *Darwin and Intelligent Design*; Haught, *God after Darwin*; Mayr, *What Evolution Is*; and Mayr and Ruse, *Darwin*

But speculation about evolution in the natural world far predates even the modern period. Ancient Greek thinkers imagined the possibility of a remote past in sometimes strikingly accurate terms.

Six centuries before the Common Era, the philosopher Anaximander (c. 610–545 B.C.E.) speculated that the world began as a watery soup with human beings as fish-like creatures slowly developing the necessary traits to become land-dwellers. While no stratum of rock has yielded human fish-like fossils, Anaximander's image of the Earth's watery beginnings appears as a verified aspect of the world's development according to modern theory. Scientists today describe the earliest fossilized bacteria, dating back some three and one-half billion years, as thriving in a deep ocean environment, a primeval chemical soup.

Anaximander's idea that species would undergo an entire transformation over the course of generations has its counterpart in the modern scientific conception of descent with modification.

A century later, the Greek scientist Empedocles (c. 495–435 B.C.E.) imagined the world's development in stages, with plants appearing first, then animals. Modern scientists confirmed changes like this by fossil evidence. From single-

---

and Design. The National Academy of Science (http.//www.nas.edu) has research papers and other resources on evolution and creationism at http://www.nasonline.org/site/. The Center for Science Education (NCSE) offers a thorough introduction, "Understanding Evolution for Teachers," on their website at http://www.ncseweb.org/. A recent analysis of the Intelligent Design movement is the position paper from the Office of Public Policy in the Center for Inquiry by Forrest, "Understanding the Intelligent Design Creationist Movement: Its True Nature and Goals."

cell life dated at nearly four billion years, the fossil record shows complex cells emerging some two billion years ago. The first multicellular life dates from about a billion years ago, in a time, now called the Cambrian Period, of incredible expansion in the complexity and diversity of living things. Layers of fossils reveal evolutionary stages more complex and numerous than Empedocles imagined, but his idea that living things emerged in stages anticipated Charles Darwin by more than twenty centuries.

The point is not that the Greeks knew everything but that human beings have been imagining an evolutionary past and process for millennia. Even the idea of descent with modification was not new with Darwin. His enduring achievement was to explain how such descent works.

With evidence of the fossil record, the judgment that Earth has had a long and complex history was unavoidable. Darwin applied this insight directly to life itself: *biology has a history*. It is the history of organisms in their origin, diversity, and flourishing. It is also a history of extinction and disappearance.

Two interrelated questions challenged Darwin. The first was about the fact itself: *Why evolution?* The second regarded the process: *How does evolution work?* Even with the incredible advances of the sciences over the last century, Darwin's response to each question remains at the center of the way scientists understand evolution today.

THE EMERGENCE OF SCIENTIFIC EXPLANATIONS

Darwin was one of two nineteenth-century naturalists, or biologists, to grasp the mechanism of evolution. The other was a fellow English biologist, Alfred Russell Wallace. Wallace and Darwin each arrived independently at the idea of natural selection. They were encouraged to present their findings together in scientific papers and did. They each presented findings in scientific papers in 1858. Darwin published his ground-breaking book the next year.

Oddly enough, the insights of both naturalists into biological evolution were prompted by an essay on poverty by an economist, Thomas Malthaus. Malthaus argued that any policy designed to help the poor was doomed because of the pressures created by population growth. The problem of population in the human realm turned the attention of Darwin and Wallace to the environment. What pressures did the environment bring on animal species? What effect does the environment have on populations of organisms? Why do populations sometimes grow by leaps and bounds? What limits some groups within the same population but not others?

These questions proved to be key to the insight into evolution for both Darwin and Wallace: What role does environment play in the survival of species? The title Darwin gave to his book previewed his answer: *The Origin of Species by Means of Natural Selection.*

To account for the origin of species by means of an empirical cause, natural selection, contrasted with the way in which the ancient Greeks, Christian theologians, and earlier scientists had long accounted for the world. In different ways they all grounded the origin in a *supernatural* cause. For Plato, as we saw earlier, the world is the work of a demiurge, an artisan or craftsman who orders the world from preexisting material. Aristotle accounted for the movement from potentiality to actuality of things by the idea of a Prime Mover.

This supernatural kind of argument remained compelling even into the modern period. As Christian theologians and scientists attributed the existence of things to a transcendent God, they argued in turn that the design of the world demonstrated God's existence. The Greek word *telos* means purpose or end. A *teleological argument* reasons from the order of the world to the mind behind it. It highlights features of the world—its order, design, complexity—that point to a transcendent source. The potentiality of things to become what they are is put in terms of finality—the nature of each thing "heads toward" the actuality created for it by God. God is the final and transcendent end toward which the potentiality of the whole universe heads.

The medieval theologian Thomas Aquinas had developed a teleological argument as the fifth of his five proofs for God. He argued that things that are unknowing and act toward an end must be directed toward this end by a being with intelligence. From this he draws a conclusion: "Therefore some intelligent being exists by whom all natural things are directed to their end; and this being we call God."[2]

Despite critiques from David Hume and Immanuel Kant, teleology reigned. The most influential work at the time of Darwin was William Paley's *Natural Theology* (1802). Paley drew on a watchmaker analogy that dated back to Cicero, the Roman statesman and philosopher who lived in the century before the Common Era (c. 106–43 C.E.), and which was used by others, among them the experimental scientist of the sixteenth century, Robert Hooker, and the famous philosopher René Descartes of the seventeenth century. Paley's conclu-

2. Aquinas, *Summa Theologica* I, q2, art. 3.

sion was confident: the marks of design are too strong to be dismissed. Design requires a designer. The designer must be a person. That person is God.[3] Just as the design of a watch implies its intelligent designer, a watchmaker, so the structure and complexity of things point to a transcendent designer of the universe. The marvelous features of the universe could not be accidental. The wings of birds, the fins of fish, the relation of bee and flower, the human eye—these things are the way they are because of God's will, purpose, and end for them. Such intricacy and complexity as the world exhibits must be grounded in a supernatural cause.

The only alternative to a transcendent designer, Paley thought, was *chance*. But surely chance could not provide what appears to be a beneficial design to the way different species are constructed and the interrelation of things with one another. Christian theologians and scientists alike rejected the idea that random chance could account for these features of the world. How but through God could something so exquisitely formed as the human eye have come into being?

But perfection and purpose are not the whole story. Along with the exquisite and beautiful, the universe has its share of the distasteful and ugly, the weird and horrific, the *imperfect*. What is to be made of a transcendent designer who creates a species with wings but which does not fly? Or what of the creation of a species of fish whose habitat in pitch black caves deep on the ocean floor makes its eyes irrelevant? The mating pattern of some species qualifies as horrific, at least for the victim: some female spiders are so aggressive that they eat the male after he has contributed his sperm in their

3. Paley, *Natural Theology.*

mating ritual. The behavior of the female fishing spider is beyond aggressive. She sometimes eats her male suitor *before* he has a chance to even attempt to fertilize her eggs. What kind of designer conceived of the potentiality of this nature? Enlightenment figures, notably David Hume, challenged the teleological argument by pointing out that perfect design is hardly the last word about the actual world that exists.

Darwin initially found Paley's natural theology compelling. But gradually he rejected its adequacy as a *scientific* explanation. The question is not about God's existence. That is not a question for scientists to determine. A supernatural explanation is deficient because it cannot be empirically verified. God is not an object or event in the world of objects and events that can be subject to repeated experiments. The essential criterion of a genuinely scientific explanation is verification.

Paley could account for the positive and good in the universe as a product of God. He had a harder time with the negative and evil. Darwin took up this problem. Francisco Ayala writes that "Darwin's *Origin of Species* is, first and foremost, a sustained effort to solve Paley's conundrum of how to account scientifically for the design of organisms, but also for their imperfections, dysfunctions, oddities, and cruelties."[4]

Rejecting the idea that God intervenes in the world to create species, Darwin grounded design empirically. As Ayala points out, for Darwin design refers to the adaptations and behaviors resulting from what he called natural selection:

> As a consequence of natural selection, organisms exhibit design, that is, adaptive organs and functions, but it is not "intelligent" design, imposed by

4. Ayala, *Darwin and Intelligent Design*, 12.

God as a Supreme Engineer. Rather it is the result
of a natural process of selection, promoting the
adaptation of organisms to their environments.
Individuals that have beneficial variations—ones
that improve their probability of survival and
reproduction—leave more descendants than do
individuals of the same species that have less beneficial variations.[5]

"Design" implies purpose and a plan at work. "Adaption" is a
functional term. Things develop traits that meet demands of
their environment, not by virtue of a plan unfolding and an
inherent purpose but because organisms continually adapt to
the environment. Evolution is the consequence of adaptation.
Citing *The Origin of Species*, Ayala writes: "In nature, over
generations, Darwin's argument continues, favorable variations will be preserved, multiplied and conjoined; injurious
ones will be eliminated. In one place, Darwin avers: 'I can
see no limit to this power [natural selection] in slowly and
beautifully *adapting* each form to the most complex relations
of life.'"[6]

Identifying the Mechanisms of Evolution

Prior to Wallace and Darwin, scientists acknowledged the fact
of evolution but were not yet able to identify the mechanism
of evolutionary process. What could account for features of
the world such as these?

5. Ibid., 12.
6. Ibid., 15.

- Change in descent from ancestors
- Variation in the population of an organism
- The incredible diversity of organisms
- The flourishing of an organism
- The failure of an organism to thrive
- The disappearance of organisms completely

Darwin focused his attention on variations within populations of organisms and the fact that variations are inherited. It goes without saying that reproduction is crucial to the survival of a population. Reproduction is not assured. When organisms cannot meet challenges presented by the environment, their own survival is threatened. What offspring they have start with the same disadvantage.

Species thrive that have traits that enable them to find food efficiently, to escape from predators by running or swimming quickly, and to withstand the extreme temperatures their environment might impose on them. Genetic mutations produce new traits. Not all are beneficial. But some are advantageous. They help to meet particular demands of the environment. The new trait raises the probabilities for survival, and with survival, reproduction. It is inherited by their offspring. This "natural selection," Darwin argued, is the mechanism of evolution. Talking about the environment "naturally selecting" species with the most advantageous traits makes the environment appear aggressive or intentional. But the environment is not an active agent. An example of two birds of different colors is instructive.

A bird whose color blends in with the green of trees is at less risk from predators than one whose color makes it stand out dramatically against the dark forest background. If predators cannot see green birds, they cannot eat them. By virtue of having escaped being eaten, the chances for the green birds' survival are already up and reproduction an actuality. In contrast, the offspring of white birds may be few and far between because predators easily locate white objects against the dark green forest. White birds get eaten. The probabilities for offspring fall to zero. Eaten birds have no offspring. The white bird population grows smaller or disappears completely.

Being green contributes to survival, and survival to the reproduction of green offspring. *Being white* is a virtual invitation to extinction. What occurred first as a genetic mutation—green feathers—becomes a common trait as it is inherited and enhanced over generations of green birds reproducing. The environment "naturally selects" green birds over white birds, meaning, greenness is an advantageous trait that contributes not only to the survival of green birds but to the dominance of this population of birds over those who lack this trait.

Natural selection is the *how* of evolution. It is the natural cause of a natural phenomenon. In identifying it as a principal means of evolution, Darwin accounted for evolution with an empirically-based explanation. While not all scientists were quite on board with the exigencies of modern scientific method at Darwin's time, his work gave greater impulse to the matter of empirical evidence. If the explanation is to be scientific, it must appeal only to what has been tested and verified in whatever data are relevant to the inquiry. Thus the exclusion of an appeal to the supernatural as a properly scientific explanation.

The discovery of genes and their role in inheritance deepened and completed Darwin's insight into natural selection as the mechanism of evolution. The essential contribution was from the nineteenth-century work of the monk Gregor Mendel (1822–84). He demonstrated genetic heredity by meticulous documentation of how probabilities governed the passing along of traits that are "dominant" or "recessive" in the parents. His work was not recognized during his life.

The connection of natural selection with genetics was made by the twentieth-century geneticist Theodosius Dobzhansky (1900–1975) in his landmark book, *Genetics and the Origin of Species* (1937). The unification of Dobzhansky's work with Darwin's is referred to as the "modern synthesis." Evolution was then understood as a *genetic change* in a population. Adaptations to the environment by way of mutations of genes are the source of descent with modification in organisms.

With the discoveries by Francis Crick (1916–2004) and James D. Watson (b. 1928) in 1943, the specific structure of genes and the site of their variation was identified as DNA in the nucleus of a cell. It carries genetic information and forms the basis of inheritance.[7] DNA is a nucleic acid, a complex organic compound found in all cells. It constitutes the chemical substance of genes.

The "double helix" image of the internal structure of DNA—a twisted ladder of two strands of four repeating nucleotides or bases—is one of the most famous images from

7. One resource for information about molecules is Reciprocal Net, funded by the U.S. National Science Foundation. See the page on common molecules at http://www.reciprocalnet.org/edumodules/commonmolecules/index.html.

contemporary science. These bases contain all the information needed for self-replication and continuation of life. Their specific sequence determines individual hereditary characteristics.

Mutations occur at random all the time. They are the source of genetic diversity and the raw material for new species. If the gene variant gives the organism an advantage in its environment, as we suggested above, those who have it will be more likely to survive and reproduce successfully.

Subsequent to Darwin, further mechanisms of evolution have been identified. *Genetic drift* is an example. The more descendents individuals leave, the more of their genetic make-up they leave. The descendent group is genetically stronger than others, not because it is healthier or has any other advantage, but simply because of unchallenged reproductive success and survival. Natural selection is not random. Genetic drift is random.

SCIENTIFIC PROCEDURES

As we have seen, the fossil record documents change in organisms. Fossil layers reveal the emergence of new species and transitional organisms between the old and new species. Some species disappear from the record. This process raises questions. Why do organisms change? Why do they become extinct? Why do new species emerge?

Even into the modern period, despite the rise of modern empirical science, scientists often answered these questions with supernatural explanations. Just as laws of nature communicate God's will, changes in geological formations or in the design of species reflect God's intervention. Increasingly, modern scientists have restricted their explanations of natural phenomena without recourse to a cause that lies outside the empirical order.

The issue here did not have to do with the existence of God or belief in God. The issue is verification. The fundamental requirement of modern science is that hypotheses be checked by a return to the data. Have the conditions been met for x to be the case? Verified judgments are the building blocks of scientific knowledge. When we assert, "This is true," we are making the claim that we have verified our judgment of x.

Because God is not a finite datum, an object or event among objects and events within the world, God cannot be verified empirically. The supernatural explanation, *God caused x*, cannot be checked against any evidence.

Darwin made a methodological move that rendered his theory of the mechanism of evolution truly modern. He bracketed God as an explanation and confined his understanding of how and why evolution works to the natural order. For the *why* of evolution Darwin argued that the *relationship* between organisms and their environment was primary. Adaptation is *why* organisms evolve. Successful adaptations increase longevity, which in turn raises the probabilities for reproductive success. The survival of offspring and their reproduction assures the survival of the species itself.

The sheer facticity of an environment demands that organisms, if they are not to perish and disappear, adapt to its features. Beneficial adaptations to these particularities is the concrete and necessary solution to the problem of their existence. Success in meeting environmental challenges is essential for each organism's survival.

That organisms adapt to their environment is a foundational principle of evolutionary theory. That they must do so further elaborates the *why* of evolution. Random mutations in the DNA structure produce the raw material for adaptive change. They are the cause of genetic diversity. But gene variations may or may not be beneficial. Inasmuch as a gene variation enables an organism more successfully to meet the demands of the environment, those who have it will be at an advantage against those without it. The inheritance of the new trait by their offspring raises the probabilities for the next generation's survival.

By locating the mechanism for evolution in nature, Darwin eliminated the implicit difficulty inherent in Paley's natural theology. The imperfection and dysfunction we find in the world present problems for one's conception of divine power, wisdom, or goodness. What kind of God thinks up all these horrific mating rituals we find in spiders? But if the world we discover is a product of natural selection, our conception of God remains without threat.

Without the crucial components of analysis supplied by Darwin and subsequent scientists, Paley's account of an evolutionary world was bound to be deficient. But his work apparently sharpened Darwin's commitment to the methodological principle of modern empirical science. This methodological commitment on the part of scientists does not say anything about God's existence.

Darwin's methodological principle rejects neither God nor creation. The question of an ultimate source of the universe lies outside the boundaries of science. What Darwin explicitly rejected was not creation as the term should be understood theologically, but the term as it is used in conjunction with a literalist interpretation of Genesis 1.

The overwhelming evidence scientists cite for evolution gives rise to the assurance that, in fact, the universe has developed and changed over the course of billions of years. The scientist who has at hand a theoretical understanding of an evolutionary world and respect for the scholarly understanding of Genesis 1 as poetry and symbolic narrative will not then set Genesis 1 up to be rejected as bad science. Lest we simply argue a pseudo-conflict in the terms given by fundamentalists, a critical distinction must be maintained without fail: Genesis 1 is not science to begin with, but proclamation and praise.

As we saw in chapter 1, the writer's concern was existential: Would the discouraged and grief-stricken exiles in Babylon remain loyal to Yahweh? Trying to keep the people faithful, the writer portrays God as all-powerful and all-knowing. God is good and the product of God's choice and decision—the universe—is good. Surely the writer would have been surprised if his narrative was used to answer an entirely different question: "What happened?"

In addition, as we emphasized in the preface and chapter 2, the theological concept of *creation* is different than the idea of *special creation* used by fundamentalists. It is an answer to questions that complement—not duplicate—the questions raised by the natural sciences. "Why is the universe here?" or "Why is the universe intelligible?" are philosophical or theological questions about *being*. As Darwin signaled in the title of his book, evolutionary theory regards the origin of species, not the origin of existence, or as others sometimes say, the origin of life. Darwin rejected any appropriation of Genesis

1 as relevant to understanding the natural world in properly scientific and theoretical terms. The notions of *special creation* and the *fixity of species* belong to pre-evolutionary science and, in theology, are linked to an inappropriate use of Genesis 1 as science and history.

The scientific consensus is that the evidence for evolution is incontrovertible. And among developed nations, the population of the United States is alone in its resistance to evolution. Why does evolutionary theory cause so much of a problem for ordinary people? Confusion and misunderstanding about scientific method, hypothesis, and theory are significant contributors to the problem. We will treat each briefly.

SCIENTIFIC METHOD

We see a natural desire to know that issues forth in the questions of children and throughout our lives in the back-and-forth of ordinary living.[8] Our common sense represents the cumulative set of judgments resulting from both our own self-correcting process of learning and that of our culture. I understand things one way or another because my cultural world understands them that way. If I move to another culture, "the way things are" might not be quite the same. In my context, I know enough about things to make intelligent conversation and to negotiate my way in interpersonal meetings. What I know, I know in relation to me. "It's hot" means just that—that I feel hot, the house is hot, the outside heat is brutal—but no more. What "hot" means in terms of a technical definition of *temperature* is not of particular interest to me

8. I draw from the work of Lonergan here.

in the common-sense mode. Unless something drastic like dementia occurs to me, my common sense develops with experience. It is the language with which we each talk of politics and business, family affairs, sports, and international affairs.

Common sense is intelligent yet it has its limitations. Some people want to explain temperature, not just how a hot day feels to them. In our spontaneous desire to know is a pull to understand things, not just in relation to me but "in relation to themselves." We want to understand something—like Mount Everest—simply because it is there to be understood. This further understanding—theory—is like common sense, in that it is a self-correcting process of learning, but it is more deliberative and methodical. Both common sense and theoretical knowing are a compound of the internal activities of experiencing, understanding, and judging. For both kinds of knowing, knowledge of reality is dependent on correct judgments of fact.

While theory is not limited to the natural sciences, all fields in the sciences are theoretical. What one understands scientifically, one understands "in itself" rather than "for me." Claims are backed by evidence. Insights into data generate ideas formulated in testable hypotheses. A return to the data for further testing and experimentation yields a judgment: *This is so.* There are conditions for saying that *x is so.* When we affirm those conditions are fulfilled, we can make the judgment: *x is so.* What we mean by truth is verified judgments.

The goal of theoretical thinking differs from that of common sense. If the primary aim of common sense is living, the aim of theoretical thinking is knowing. Real, thorough *knowing* is the product of long and intensive labor. It is the work of years in research labs or out in the field. Those engaged in theory write dissertations and scientific papers. Often the language of theorists is mathematical. In this systematic realm of meaning, terms are defined and precision is valued. Common sense describes; theory explains. Articulate in the lab and the classroom, those involved in theoretical understanding might be momentarily paralyzed when visiting the hometown coffee shop and someone asks, "Now, just what is it you do?"

This development from common sense knowing to technical knowing is a development of *mind*. Consciousness becomes differentiated. Where there was one realm of meaning, common sense, now there are two realms of meaning, common sense and theory. Theoretical thinking is a new way of knowing. The person whose consciousness is differentiated can go back and forth between common sense and theory. But precisely because it is *undifferentiated*, undifferentiated consciousness cannot understand *differentiated* consciousness. Common sense misunderstands theory. It trivializes theory, describing it as just a guess or a hunch or even a deception or conspiracy against common sense. There can be a kind of arrogance, as well, in common sense, asserting that it knows what there is to be known over against "just a theory."

From a common sense standpoint, theory looks like too many words or too complicated a set of numbers. In this description of "evolutionists" by a person identified with creationism there is no clue that scientific theory is a technical understanding of something: "Another problem, which adds to the student's frustration, is the overuse of scientific jargon and unpronounceable words, burying him in a sea of confusion. Typically, evolutionists will have the tendency to redefine commonly used terms to mean something else. This is called *obfuscation*, and it is a tactic that is not only used against creationists, but it is used to create a general state of insanity."[9] Another person, exhibiting the frustration of common sense thinking when confronted by the complexity of theoretical mathematics, wrote: "Another particularly virulent strain of this disease is the paper which is made up of nothing but mathematical equations strung together by 'and' and 'therefore' with incomprehensible charts and graphs."[10]

THE NATURE OF SCIENCE

One of the chief contributors to the success of creationists in undermining evolution is that so many people do not understand what scientists are doing. "Scientific method" sounds ominous. The methodological principle of excluding the supernatural and explaining everything according only to the natural sounds suspiciously like atheism.

One operative factor in the ignorance or misunderstanding of science is the difference we introduced above between common sense and theoretical understanding. Scientific method is one instance of the latter.

Scientific method is the method of the human mind "writ large," so to speak. It follows the way our minds work. Like a wheel we move from data not yet understood to questions for understanding to insights into the data. The understanding we formulate into a hypothesis is then itself a object of inquiry. Is it correct? Do we understand the data correctly? Before we can say that what we understand is true, we have to return to the data to confirm what we understand. The hy-

9. Sharp, "Advice to Christians Who Must Deal with Evolutionists." See the creationist website: http://www.rae.org/advice/html.
10. Ibid.

pothesis is a testable formulated idea. A scientific hypothesis should: (1) link and explain different phenomena, (2) point to further discoveries, and (3) be capable of being tested. When we are able to verify the hypothesis with evidence, then we can make the claim of truth. A theory is such a claim, an interlocking set of verified hypotheses. It is the product of verified judgments.

A hypothesis that is not subject to testing cannot be a scientific explanation. Claims to understand the natural world that start from authority, for example, instead of data, are masquerading as scientific inquiry. Those who oppose evolution from a religious point of view portray the Bible as a scientific authority. But even if it were such an authority, it still would constitute a misplaced starting point. Scientific understanding starts with data and is verified as true or false by way of evidence provided by the data.

Linus Pauling, a Nobel Prize-winning biochemist, said of science: "Science is the search for truth."[11] The whole of the natural world is the arena for this search. What we discover, we can explain. Truth is understanding correctly.

Science is never completed. What we presently understand becomes the foundation for new questions. New data and new questions keep scientific knowledge on the move. This lack of completeness is not a defect in science but a consequence of the self-correcting process of learning that characterizes both common sense and theory. Just as "descent with modification" occurs in the natural world as changes in species, so, too, in human consciousness, new data evoke new questions. New insights bring about changes in our un-

11. Pauling, *No More War!*

derstanding. Revision is an intrinsic dimension of scientific knowing. Human knowledge evolves because there is something further to be understood. While our capacity for raising questions is unrestricted, our understanding is incremental and restricted. We never have the full grasp of everything there is to be understood.

STATUS AND VALUE OF EVOLUTIONARY THEORY

In the order of being, evolution is a *fact*. Evolution is a primary feature of the world we discover. In the order of knowing, evolution is a *theory*. It is the technical understanding of the development of diversity and complexity in the physical world. In the sciences, it is called a unifying concept because of its explanatory power across disciplinary lines. It is the idea confirmed by evidence from a range of sciences—astronomy, biology, physics, and many others—that the universe has a history and that change has taken place. It is not simply that this concept should be taught in the sciences but that the scientific disciplines themselves cannot be adequately taught without evolution as a foundational idea for explaining the subject of each particular discipline.

Many science faculties and professional organizations include an explanation of the difference between fact and theory because the terms are misunderstood and misused so often.

The Duquesne University Biological Sciences faculty describes the difference this way.[12] On fact:

---

12. Duquesne University Department of Biological Sciences. http://www.science.duq.edu/pdf/BiolDPosPapGeneral.pdf. The statements on fact and theory below are from this document.

First, evolution is a fact. Organisms have changed over time and are related to each other by descent from common ancestors over billions of years. All organisms have adaptations that make them fit to live in their environments and these adaptations are the product of natural selection acting on random mutations in the genetic material. The evidence supporting these conclusions is so overwhelming that we can safely call them facts in every sense of that word. Those people who reject evolution as a fact are simply not conversant in any meaningful way with these data.

And on theory:

Secondly, evolution is also a theory. We use this term scientifically, meaning a comprehensive idea with great organizing and predictive power. We do not use the word in the vernacular, meaning a mere opinion. Evolutionary theory is as wide-ranging and predictive an idea as are relativity theory, quantum theory, and the theory of gravitation. It is supported by data collected over 150 years from fields as diverse as genetics, comparative morphology, developmental biology, biogeography, behavior, geology, and paleontology. No idea exists that organizes the data from these disparate fields as successfully as the theory of evolution. And yet evolution has been under attack since it was first suggested.

Darwin made *historicity* a foundational category for biology. Biology became not only the study of living organisms and their interaction with their environment but the study of the history of organisms. In reconstructing changes organisms undergo, evolutionary biology tells a story of the Earth's past. This history of change has been truly remarkable and takes place within an even larger tableau. The earliest fossilized single-cell organism dates from three and a half billion years ago. Geologists put the age of Earth at four to five billion years. The universe is thought to be ten to thirteen billion years old. Since the discoveries of Edwin Hubble in the 1920s and the conclusion that the universe is expanding, the accepted theoretical account of the development of the universe is that it began in a single explosive event.

From the empirical evidence of expansion, contemporary cosmological theory works backwards to the judgment that the universe was once incredibly small. Biological evolution brings us into the expanding universe and to the intricate development of species, including human beings. We, too, have emerged and descended with modification over a long period of time, starting from the single-cell ancestor of all organisms and preceeding to the then branching pre-human and then distinctly human species.

A century of scientific research has validated the reality of evolution. To use a favorite phrase found in the scientific literature, "the evidence is overwhelming." By the beginning of the twentieth century, just fifty years after Darwin's *Origin of Species*, scientists took evolution for granted. Still, the theory undergoes constant modification. Debate about evolution continues—not *whether* evolution has occurred, but *how* it occurs. While other mechanisms of evolution, such as genetic drift, have been identified subsequent to Darwin, his contribution of natural selection remains central to the theoretical understanding of biological evolution.

SCIENCE AND FAITH

In popular writing, it is not unusual to see science and atheism associated, as if doing science invited rejection of God.
This caricature of science is not exclusively the work of creationists, but they do their fair share of demonizing modern
science. They present evolutionary theory in particular as an
atheistic teaching responsible for a wide range of social ills
that plague modern society.

Some scientists are atheists. Richard Dawkins and
Stephen Hawking are perhaps the most prominent of those to
make their atheism a dimension of public reflection on their
scientific work. Scientists have many reasons for choosing un-
belief over belief. For some the laws of physics suffice. They do
not need the transcendent to account for the universe. Others
reject an anthropomorphic God "up there" when modern
cosmology has no "up," as did the ancient worldview.

For others there is the difficulty of integrating divine
reality into Newton's universe of classical laws, Einstein's universe of general and special relativity, and the quantum world
introduced by Max Planck. Some attribute their atheism to a
rejection of the dogmatism of religions, to the human suffering created by religious wars, and to the religious justification
of injustices, such as slavery and women's subordination, as
the "order of creation." There is no shortage of reasons for the
atheism of particular scientists. But the "naturalism of evolution" is not among the most common of reasons given.

Granted, some scientists are atheists, it is manifestly
untrue that all scientists are atheists or that engaging in evolutionary biology heads one down an atheist path. One of the
most influential spokespersons for evolution today is biolo-

gist Francisco Ayala. Dr. Ayala has emphasized the positive relation between religious faith and evolutionary theory. In numerous writings he has insisted that there is no contradiction between belief in God and affirmation of evolutionary theory.

The argument against evolution by religious conservatives is not shared by mainline Christian traditions. As Robert Pennock points out: "The Catholic Church and most mainline Protestant denominations, for instance, do not consider evolution to be in conflict with Christian faith, holding that God could have ordained the evolutionary mechanism as the process for creating the biological world."[13]

Turning the creationist accusation around, Kenneth Miller, a scientist and believer, argues that the creationists demonstrate a lack of faith in God's omnipotence because they assume that God does not have the power to create a world in which life could evolve by natural laws and must intervene to accomplish certain things.[14]

Faith is not absent from scientific inquiry in any case. Belief is an intrinsic dimension of scientists' inquiry. To engage in any investigation of physical reality requires that scientists believe that a real world exists outside of their own minds. Albert Einstein called this belief the basis of science. Scientists anticipate the rationality of the universe. Einstein adverted to his own deep sense of mystery and the "profound faith" of scientists in the intelligibility of the universe. That it can be understood by human minds evokes a sense of great awe. Scientists take for granted that both the systematic and the unsystematic can be understood, the former through

13. Pennock, "Creationism and Intelligent Design," 144.
14. Miller, *Finding Darwin's God*, 217–18, 267–69, 288–89.

classical laws and the latter as probabilities through statistical laws. When new insights challenge their worldviews and require that basic assumptions undergo radical change, as happened with relativity or with quantum theory, they remain confident that worldviews can undergo such transformation. They have *faith* that the real is intelligible and that human intelligence can know it. They have scientific faith in the human ability to grasp theoretically whatever exists in mathematical expression of its patterns and relationships.

Einstein acknowledged a sense that accompanied his scientific work. If there is something in him that is "religious," he said, it is his "unbounded admiration for the structure of the world." He portrayed science as a religious activity, calling science not only compatible with religion but dependent on it. While still a teenager, Einstein rejected the Judaeo-Christian notion of a personal God as anthropomorphic. But his initial reaction against quantum indeterminacy contains one of his best-known remarks about God: "Quantum mechanics is very impressive. But an inner voice tells me that it is not yet the real thing. The theory produces a good deal but hardly brings us to the secret of the Old One. I am at all events convinced that *He* does not play dice."[15]

The *question* of the intelligibility of the universe is a theological one: Why an intelligible world? Why a universe whose structures correspond to the human capacity to understand? The physicist and theologian John Polkinghorne gives a theological answer to the question: "Science is possible, and mathematics so remarkably effective, because the

15. The views of Einstein noted here are found in Brooke, "Einstein, God, and Time"; and Jaki, "The Role of Faith in Physics." This quote is from Brooke, "Einstein," 951.

world is a creation and we creatures are made in the image of the Creator. Fundamental physics reveals a universe shot through with signs of mind, and it is an attractive understanding that it is indeed the Mind of God that lies behind the wonderful cosmic order."[16]

16. Polkinghorne, *Traffic in Truth*, 33.

FOUR

Catholics and the Theory of Evolution

Christian reaction to the advent of evolutionary theory in the nineteenth century was divided between enthusiasm and horror.[1] The most passionate was surely Darwin's great defender, Thomas Huxley, whose self-deprecating remark may have occurred to more than one of Darwin's fellow biologists: "How stupid of me not to have thought of that!" People opposed evolutionary theory for many reasons, most commonly perhaps because of the perceived insult of human development's taking place right along with the rest of the natural world. Coming from the same watery beginnings and single-cell ancestor as other species left humans somewhere on the same familial tree as the apes. Many think that evolutionary theory impugned the special place that human beings held in the universe as well as the biblical affirmation that human beings are made in the image of God.

One new religious group was formed at least in part because of their anti-evolutionism. Theologians associated

1. For religious reactions to Darwin, see Numbers and Stenhouse, eds., *Disseminating Darwin*. See p. 10 for the reference to Charles Hodge noted below. An older study but still regarded as a "masterful synthesis" is Moore, *The Post-Darwinian Controversies*. For the Thomas Huxley quote below, see http://www.ucmp.berkeley.edu/history/thuxley.html. On Mendel, mentioned below, see Henig, *The Monk in the Garden*.

with Princeton Seminary formed a new religious movement, *Fundamentalism,* to counter Darwin's theory of evolution, liberal theology, and secularism. One of the most influential Princeton theologians, Charles Hodge, examined evolutionary theory in his book, *What Is Darwinism?* Hodge argued that Darwin's emphasis on "natural" selection was a rejection of design or final causality, that is, a rejection of God as the supernatural cause of the universe and all things within it. This alone brought it into conflict with Christianity.

THINKING OF SCIENCE

Generally, though, Protestants of various denominations did not share the fundamentalists' dismal view of evolution. Many were quite open to scientific developments. They did not find the prospect of integrating creation with evolution distasteful or impossible. Nor did they take Darwin's mechanism of evolution, natural selection, as intrinsically atheistic. *Theistic evolution* reflects this mainstream Christian position of integration. God is the ground of the universe in all its detail, including its chief feature, evolutionary process.

A distinctive and instructive history of religious conviction coming to terms with evolutionary theory can be seen in the Roman Catholic Church's reaction to Darwin's theory. Like Protestant fundamentalists, the Catholic Church initially opposed certain aspects of evolutionary biology but, unlike them, Catholics did not reject it totally. At least one difference is relevant. Fundamentalists came to Darwin with the Bible as the center of their religious faith. Evolutionary theory conflicted dramatically with the way in which fundamentalists understood creation and the history of humankind.

Catholics came to this same scientific development with the Bible, too. The fact that Catholics did not interpret the Bible in exclusively literal terms, however, made a significant difference in their eventual appropriation of evolutionary theory. Like fundamentalists, nineteenth-century Catholics presumed the historicity of the Genesis 1–3 stories of creation and sin, but their views of biblical interpretation would allow for change and accommodation of new insights. More will be said specifically about these changes below.

In addition, Catholics came to this new scientific development with a strong intellectual tradition behind them that placed a great value on reason—as found in science and elsewhere—as a real source of knowledge. Apart from revelation, human reason is capable of knowing the world. Moreover, natural reason is capable of knowing the existence of God. In the end, perhaps the greatest difference between fundamentalists and Catholics is the high regard in Catholicism for human knowledge generally and scientific knowing specifically.

Differences in Protestant and Catholic views of the effect of original sin were at work here, too. The Protestant tradition tended to think of reason as corrupted by original sin. In contrast, Catholics portrayed reason as merely darkened by original sin. While the terms "darkened" or "corrupted" might appear similar, in this context, they generate different views of human knowledge. The Catholic view can be called "optimistic" and the Protestant view "pessimistic." The Protestant understanding of original sin predisposes their theological view to be much more negative or suspicious about the capabilities of knowledge.

It is not irrelevant, either, that throughout the Catholic tradition consistent efforts have been made to integrate science and theology. One of the more famous examples is Thomas Aquinas's use of Aristotle in the Middle Ages. Some authority is given to scientific work because of the engagement of priests as trained scientists as well. In this particular case of evolutionary theory, next to Darwin's insight into natural selection, the essential contribution to understanding evolution came through insights into genetics and heredity. Gregor Mendel, who discovered the laws of inheritance that would become so important in what became known as the "modern synthesis," was an Augustinian friar from Austria.

Efforts to integrate science and theology are evident, too, in the Vatican's direct sponsorship of scientific research today. The Vatican Observatory is the oldest astronomical research institution in the world. It traces its origins to Pope Gregory XIII in 1582 and its more recent restructuring to Pope Leo XIII, who, in 1892, said that he hoped that through the Observatory's work "everyone might see clearly that the Church and her Pastors are not opposed to the true and solid science, whether human or divine, but that they embrace it, encourage it, and promote it with the fullest possible dedication."[2]

The Vatican scientists have conferences on such topics as "scientific perspectives on divine action" and "evolutionary and molecular biology." Their collaboration with the Center for Theology and the Natural Sciences in Berkeley, California, has resulted in several books, two of which are:

2. Vatican Observatory, online: http://www.vaticanstate.va/EN/Other_Institutions/The_Vatican_Observatory.htm.

Quantum Cosmology and the Laws of Nature,[3] and *Chaos and Complexity*.[4]

ACCEPTING AND REJECTING EVOLUTION

The initial rejection of evolution by the Catholic Church was based on doctrine, not on an evaluation of the evidence of the natural world that scientists presented for it. While Protestants came to their rejection from the Bible and Catholics from doctrine, in this case, their concern was the same: the relation of Adam and Eve, original sin, and evolution. The teaching office of the Catholic Church simply forbade discussion. The historicity of Adam and Eve, their first sin, and the biological inheritance of an actual sin by their descendants were not subjects open for debate. If science entertained views that differed from Catholic dogma, these views could not be accepted. What is not stated explicitly is the relation of these figures and events to the redemptive purpose of Christ.

While the magisterium or teaching authority could pronounce discussions closed, Roman Catholic theologians engaged in teaching in colleges and universities could not avoid the intellectual difficulties presented to church doctrines by advances in the evolutionary sciences. These challenges were heightened by the work of biblical scholars engaged in literary and historical-critical scholarship. The question of the historicity of Adam and Eve—and the implications for the doctrine of original sin—came up in both fields.

Protestant fundamentalists responded to this dual threat by retreating into the prescientific world of the Bible

3. Russell et al., eds., *Quantum Cosmology and the Laws of Nature*.
4. Russell et al., eds., *Chaos and Complexity*.

and declaring it normative. This choice guaranteed that their religious worldview would remain in tension with modern sciences and scholarship. Their literal interpretation of the Bible presumed the text as history. If the story presents Adam and Eve living in a garden, they historically existed and lived in a garden. No matter what story of the Earth's past was being unearthed by the research of geologists and paleontologists, fundamentalists maintained that, as revelation, the Bible is an authoritative source for history and science as well as the truths for salvation.

While Catholics did not consider the Bible a sole authority nor the literal interpretation normative, still Catholic doctrine clearly was tied to a literalist understanding of Adam and Eve. By modern times, the doctrine of original sin was taken simply as a given truth of human existence. Its origins and development had been lost to theological memory. In fact, as we saw in chapter 2, the doctrine developed over the first five centuries of Christianity in response to the question of why Christ's redemption was necessary for everyone. The notion of an inherited, actual sin, as finally formulated by Augustine, was affirmed by church councils around the fifth century, but it was not until the Council of Trent in 1563 that this idea of original sin was given dogmatic status.[5]

From the time of its emergence, the doctrine of original sin functioned as the pivot around which other Christian doctrines revolved. It was the crucial element, the unifying doctrine bringing together Christ, redemption, and the church. It answered many questions:

5. Wiley, *Original Sin*, 37–102.

- Why evil?
    - » Because of the distortion of nature brought about by original sin—people do what is irrational and irresponsible rather than rational and responsible.

- Why are human beings alienated from God?
    - » Because of original sin.

- Why did Christ come?
    - » To reconcile humanity to God by offering God's forgiveness of original sin.

- Why the church?
    - » The church exclusively mediates Christ's forgiveness of original sin.

The work of paleontologists, geologists, and other scientists disrupted this traditional doctrinal worldview, taken for granted for nearly two millennia. It was not immediately clear how this web of theological convictions could be sustained in relation to the kinds of conclusions about human origins advanced by modern scientists. This theology of redemption, in which the very purpose of the Incarnation and of the work of Christ is to remove original sin and reconcile humankind with God, is one of several ways in which redemption, the Incarnation, and Christ have been understood together. For fundamentalists, it is the exclusive way of thinking not only about redemption but the very meaning of Christianity itself.

CONCILIAR JUDGMENTS

The Catholic Church's first explicit rejection of descent with modification came a year after Charles Darwin published *The Origin of Species*. In 1860 a Catholic synod in Cologne instructed several Catholic writers to retract their views affirming *transformism*, a term they used for human evolution.[6] Transformism was judged contrary to Genesis 1–3 and to the revealed doctrine of original sin.

Ten years after publication of *The Origin of Species*, the First Vatican Council took up the question of evolutionary theory. The Council defended *monogenism* (one original set of ancestors) as a necessary truth to be believed and rejected scientific speculations about polygenism. They defended Adam as the origin of the human race and rejected dismissals of historicity. In 1909 the Pontifical Biblical Commission rejected both evolutionary theory and critical methods of biblical interpretation, insisting—because of the doctrine—on the literal interpretation of Genesis.

But, as we have seen, the church's approach to scripture underwent a fundamental transformation with the 1943 encyclical *Divino Afflante Spiritu*. The document was issued in the fiftieth anniversary year of Pope Leo XIII's encyclical *Providentissimus Deus*. In that letter Leo XIII had emphasized the need for critical methods in the study of the scriptures. The letter is described as "the supreme guide in biblical studies." The 1943 encyclical acknowledged the necessity of the work of biblical scholars for the church to understand the scriptures correctly. The premodern and prescientific character of the Bible was acknowledged and instead of retreating

6. Rahner, "Evolution," 486.

back to it, the magisterium chose to bring the scriptures into the modern world with the help of scholarship devoted to the life of the church.

While the scholarly insights into the symbolic nature of the Genesis 1–3 texts are cited in commentaries and other places, the church did not address and has not explicitly addressed the obvious question: If Adam and Eve are symbolic figures in a symbolic story, how can a *real* sin be inherited from them? Evolutionary theory was taken up again in 1950. Pope Pius XII's encyclical, *Humani Generis,* (The Origin of Humanity), shows the kind of concerns about the theory almost a century after Darwin.[7] Evolution is accepted with caution and with important distinctions. The encyclical affirms that evolution and God are not contradictory. But the encyclical also emphasizes that evolutionary theory can be used to oppose the existence of God. In a remark indicating the political divisions of a Cold War era, Pius XII writes that some support the idea of continual evolution enthusiastically: "Communists gladly subscribe to this opinion so that, when the souls of men have been deprived of every idea of a personal God, they may the more efficaciously defend and propagate their dialectical materialism."

The crucial point in the encyclical regarded the condition for acceptance or rejection of scientific theories, namely, their conformity to dogma. This position was explicit: "If any such conjectural opinions are directly or indirectly opposed to the doctrine revealed by God, then the demand that they be recognized can in no way be admitted."

7. Pope Pius XII, *Humani Generis,* 181.

Humani Generis distinguished between truths and opinions: (1) doctrines are *truths* assured by revelation; (2) scientific theories are *opinions* to be rejected if they do not coincide with revealed truths. Catholic scientists and theologians were free to inquire into human evolution, but they were prohibited from acceptance of a scientific theory of human origins that did not begin with a single pair of ancestors. The encyclical rejects polygenism, the hypothesis that humankind has descended from an original group of humans. The prohibition followed from the intrinsic relation between monogenism and original sin:

> When, however, there is question of another conjecturalism, the children of the Church by no means enjoy such liberty. For the faithful cannot embrace that opinion which maintains either that after Adam there existed on this earth true men who did not take their origin through natural generation from him as from the first parent of all or that Adam represents a certain number of first parents. Now it is in no way apparent how such an opinion can be reconciled with that which the sources of revealed truth and the documents of the Teaching Authority of the Church propose with regard to original sin, which proceeds from a sin committed by an individual Adam and which through generation is passed on to all and is in everyone as his own.

Later theologians would distinguish between what the church has taught about original sin and the historicity of Adam and Eve. It is not the latter that the Council of Trent in the sixteenth century defined as dogma but the universal sinfulness of humankind and the need for forgiveness and reconciliation with God.

Fundamental changes in the Catholic Church's position on evolution were evident in a 1996 address by Pope John Paul II to the Pontifical Academy of Sciences.[8] The pope referred to evolution as "more than a hypothesis." The title of his talk, "Truth Cannot Contradict Truth," expressed the central points the pope wanted to make. Faith should never fear any scientific finding, he argued, even one that upsets cherished views. If scripture and science conflict, a solution must be found because, as the title asserts, truth cannot contradict truth. The solution would be found, presumably, in the church's interpretation of scripture. To claim that evolution implies the absence of God, the pope emphasized, is unwarranted. Given the attention to original sin in earlier statements on evolutionary theory, it is noteworthy that John Paul II said nothing in this 1996 address about Adam and Eve or original sin.

John Paul II did demur, however, at including the human soul in the process of evolution governed by the mechanism identified by Charles Darwin, natural selection. He emphasized that the soul is divinely created. Pope Pius XII made the same point in *Humani Generis* in 1950. While the body evolves, the human soul is immediately created by God.

John Paul II's successor, Pope Benedict XVI, addressed the topic of evolution in a 2007 talk to Italian priests. He, too, rejected the tendency to present evolution as if it were in contradiction to God. Evolutionary theory is true, but it does not answer all questions, especially the classic philosophical ones:

8. A good source for Pope John Paul II is Russell et al., eds., *John Paul II on Science and Religion*.

From where does everything come? Why is there anything at all? These are questions properly addressed in other disciplines. In essence, the position of theistic evolution taken by most mainline Protestant churches has also been adopted by the Catholic Church.

The question of the relation between divine purpose and the descent of all forms of life from a common ancestor through genetic variation and natural selection was raised in a 2004 Vatican statement on creation and evolution issued by the International Theological Commission, "Communion and Stewardship: Human Persons Created in the Image of God." The Commission's statement accepted the truth of evolutionary theory but emphasized that a truly contingent natural process is not incompatible with divine purpose. To understand their complementary relation we have to take into account the difference between divine causality and created causality.

To some, the Commission members wrote, a contingent natural process is evidence of the absence of God. But from the perspective of the church's philosophical tradition, the integrity of the natural process is itself ordained by God. The document quotes the medieval theologian Thomas Aquinas: "The effect of divine providence is not only that things should happen somehow, but that they should happen either by necessity or by contingency. Therefore, whatsoever divine providence ordains to happen infallibly and of necessity happens infallibly and of necessity, and that happens from contingency, which the divine providence conceives to happen from contingency."[9]

9. Vatican Statement on Creation and Evolution, 2004. International Theological Commission, "Communion and Stewardship: Human

The Catholic Church has rejected some aspects of evolutionary theory, but more importantly it has engaged the question of the relation between theology and science. What is the proper role or arena of inquiry for each? It is proper to the work of scientists, for example, to name genetic variation and natural selection as mechanisms of evolution. But scientists go beyond the framework of their scientific discipline and method in making such claims as that there is no purpose to the universe, that human beings have no special role or meaning within it, or that God has no relation to an evolving universe. For scientists to infer that genetic variation and natural selection are unguided by God goes beyond what, as scientists, they can legitimately affirm or deny. The church is clear that the truths which scientists affirm about the natural world do not contradict the truths affirmed by the church. While not all the particulars have been addressed specifically, the principle is that faith and reason are not in opposition. Acceptance of evolution is consistent with the church's teachings.[10]

Persons Created in the Image of God." Online: http://www.bringyou .to/apologetics/p80.htm.

10. For books that bring theology and science together, see Haught, a theologian who has been a major Catholic contributor to this discussion, *God after Darwin*; idem, *Responses to 101 Questions on God and Evolution*. Also notable is Miller, a scientist, in *Perspectives on an Evolving Creation*.

FIVE

Creationism in the Public Arena

In this chapter we explore creationism and its originating religious movement, Protestant fundamentalism. The public and political activity of creationists takes place within the context of public education—science classrooms, school boards, and state education boards. Their success in resisting evolutionary theory shows in the numbers of Americans who would never identify themselves as fundamentalists but who, in polls and surveys, give the same answers to questions as fundamentalists do about, for example, the dating of the universe or the creation of human beings.

Creationism has changed names several times in the last century. In the current stage, Intelligent Design (ID) is equivalent to creationism, though without the latter's explicit biblical emphasis. ID still refuses to restrict scientific explanations to natural causes that can and must be verified to be accepted. Scientific method explicitly rules out explanations that appeal to the supernatural, to God. To fundamentalists this restriction is atheism. They do not see its value as a methodological principle necessary for scientific explanation to be a genuine contribution to our knowledge of the natural world.

We will start with some strong criticisms of fundamentalism and then turn to a description of some of its features and the role of creationism. Our discussion will include an overview of some of the more influential court cases in which creationism has been ruled an unconstitutional violation of the separation of church and state.

Critics of creationism define it harshly. R. Scott Appleby describes it as an "organized, militant religious opposition to secular modernity and its accomplices (pluralism, relativism, feminism)."[1] Peter Hodgson provides an even more sweeping condemnation: "Fundamentalism rejects critical reason and empirical evidence in favor of an ideological and sometimes fanatical faith that horribly distorts the biblical and theological principles to which it appeals. It supports a politics that is driven by aggression, fear, and xenophobia, and a culture that is intolerant of diversity, minority rights, and free inquiry."[2]

Barbara Forrest cautions against casually dismissing fundamentalist creationism and the related Intelligent Design (ID) movement: "There is widespread popular misunderstanding of the true nature and goals of the ID creationist movement. In order to counteract it effectively, an accurate understanding of its nature and agenda is imperative. The conception of ID as non-biblical and of its status as an alternative scientific theory—a conception based in ID proponents'

---

1. Appleby, "History in the Fundamentalist Imagination," 498. This article is a good introduction to the worldview shared by fundamentalists. See also Appleby and Marty, "Fundamentalism." They are the editors of the five-volume work, *The Fundamentalism Project*. Among resources for this chapter and sources for further reading is Barr, *Fundamentalism*. This book is described by some as a starting point for understanding fundamentalism although much has been written since its publication. See also Nielsen, *Fundamentalism, Mythos and World Religions*.

2. Hodgson, *Liberal Theology*, 82.

self-description, which has echoed throughout the popular media—is wrong."[3]

Fundamentalism has its roots in a theological resistance to modernity. It is not an ancient tradition but a twentieth-century religious movement and the most conservative of Protestant traditions. Donald Dayton locates the emergence of fundamentalism in the contrast between two theological orientations in early twentieth-century Protestantism, "post-millennialism" and "dispensationalism."[4] Each is an interpretation of history.

Postmillennial theology holds that Christ will reign for an era (the millennium) through a gradual acceptance of the gospel and the changed lives of those who accept it. It is a literal interpretation of the Lord's Prayer: "Your will be done on earth, as it is in heaven." The kingdom of God

3. Forrest, "Understanding the Intelligent Design Creationist Movement," 2. Forrest argues that Intelligent Design is creationism under a new name. I take this view here, too. Where does all this lead? ID is connected with the Discovery Institute and the Center for Science and Culture in Seattle, Washington. Their "Wedge Strategy" identified their goals as seeing "intelligent design theory as the dominant perspective in science; to see design theory applied in specific fields, including molecular biology, biochemistry, paleontology, physics, and cosmology in the natural sciences and ethics, politics, theology, and philosophy in the humanities; to see its influence in the fine arts; and to see design theory permeate our religious, cultural, moral, and political life."

The Wedge Strategy is quoted in many places. See, for example, the statement signed by the Duquesne University Department of Biological Sciences. Online: http://www.science.duq.edu/pdf/BiolDPos PapGeneral.pdf.

4. Dayton, "Creationism in Twentieth-Century America." The terms *postmillennialism* and *dispensationalism* are explained in Dayton and the following resources: Sandeen, *The Rise of Fundamentalism*; and Smith, "Postmillennialism and the Work of Renewal in the Theology of Jonathan Edwards."

will be realized through the work of the church. The names of B. B. Warfield and R. J. Rushdoony (noted in this chapter with Christian Reconstructionism) are associated with two different interpretations of this theology. The belief that Jesus' Second Coming will return after the millennium is the reason for the prefix *post-*. With the idea that the forces of Satan will be defeated and good will triumph over evil, this theology suggests the possibility of progress. For some mainline Protestant traditions, postmillennial ideas contributed to the assimilation of evolutionary theory.

Dispensationalism is a theology of history in which history is envisioned as seven "administrations" or stages of God's dealings with humankind between creation and the second coming of Christ in judgment. It emphasizes differences between Israel and the Church and between law and grace. It is also anti-evolutionist. It is from this theology that the idea emerges of the "rapture of the church at Christ's coming." Christ's coming will establish a worldwide kingdom.

This theology is associated with Dwight L. Moody. It was developed in the "prophecy conferences" after the Civil War, such as the Niagara Bible Conferences, popularized in the Bible School movement, and canonized in the notes of the *Scofield Bible*. This study Bible, annotated by Cyrus I. Scofield, was first published in 1909 and revised in 1917. The 1917 edition is still published by Oxford University Press. The words of Jesus are marked in red.

Dispensationalist theology is also connected with John Nelson Moody. Moody taught that God has different requirements for people in different ages and that some parts of the Bible are not obligatory for believers today. Since divine judgment is ahead, it is necessary to be born again before the return of Christ. Scofield's Bible is credited with the conviction of fundamentalists that the earth is young. The notes included the calculation of the date of creation as 4004 B.C.E., a date proposed by Archbishop James Ussher. It is also credited with generating creationism.

Dispensationalist theology is accepted by some in various Protestant churches but not by Christian traditions such as Roman Catholicism.

FEATURES OF FUNDAMENTALISM

Those involved in the beginning of fundamentalism were as opposed to liberal Protestant theology as they were to Darwin's evolutionary theory. The movement was propelled by theologians from various denominations associated with Princeton Theological Seminary. Its name came from the 1909 publication of twelve books by Reuben Archer Torrey, *The Fundamentals*, that defined the central beliefs of Christianity as Torrey saw them. The emphasis was on right belief, orthodoxy. Among the fundamental beliefs noted, these five held special importance:

- the inerrancy of the Bible
- the Virgin Birth
- the historicity of Christ's miracles
- the substitutionary atonement of Christ, and
- Christ's bodily resurrection.

The "inerrancy of the Bible" meant the truth of the Bible as a historically factual narrative. Fundamentalists read Genesis 1, the first creation story, as the revelation of an act whereby God made things essentially as they are today. By "creation," fundamentalists mean "special creation," the belief that everything came directly from God. Inerrancy also means that the Bible contains no errors in history or science, including the inferred age of the universe of about 6,000 years.

The authority of the Bible is grounded in the authority of God. Fundamentalism is patriarchal in worldview. The world is structured hierarchically, with God as its head and humankind obedient to God, and with man as the head of woman. Cultural gender patterns are regarded as the order of creation. Just as there is a "fixity of species" in creation, so there is a "fixity of gender roles" in the social world. The separate and unequal gender spheres that characterize the ancient world in which the Bible originated are taken to be normative for today as well. The public sphere is male; the private, domestic sphere is female.

In their deepest desire, fundamentalists would reestablish the religious foundation for American society that they believe once existed and that modernity destroyed. By "religious foundation" they do not intend respect and inclusion of diverse religious traditions but specifically a Christian foundation, and more specifically, the theologically conservative one shaped by the founders of the movement.

This goal, if it were to be realized, would forego one of the principal values underlying democratic society, namely the constitutional separation of church and state. The First Amendment of the U.S. Constitution guarantees the autonomy of religion. The government maintains a position of neutrality that supports religious pluralism, not exclusivism. The diversity of religions is respected, all are considered legitimate, and the government privileges none. As a theological position, religious pluralism affirms that different religions offer genuine ways of salvation for their adherents. As a political position, pluralism allows all but does not endorse any religious expression.

By contrast, fundamentalists are politically and theologically exclusivist. Reasoning from the authority of the Bible, fundamentalists are exclusivist in their understanding of salvation. Christ is the one means of salvation, as this text from the Acts of the Apostles asserts: "There is salvation in no one else, for there is no other name under heaven given among mortals by which we must be saved" (Acts 4:12).

Fundamentalists have no problem with violating the separation of church and state. They would like for the government not only to privilege Christianity but to be Christian. If there is one way to God, the value of religious diversity is lessened. They are exclusivist even in their view of other Christian denominations—not all are salvific, in fact, there may be only one that is: their own.

In this regard, the most extreme of Christian conservative groups is the Christian Reconstructionists. Its founder, Rousas John Rushdooney (1916–2001), wanted to create a theocracy by replacing constitutional law with a form of biblical law. Obviously, in a theocracy there is no separation of church and state. In contrast to the political affirmation of religious pluralism, one religion is privileged. Although small in numbers, this movement has been influential in the political power of the Christian Right over the last half century.

THE MASTER NARRATIVE

In its twelve volumes, *The Fundamentals* had space not only to identify the foundational beliefs to be accepted but also to specify what was to be rejected. Roman Catholicism was prominent on this list, as were socialism and modern philosophy. Sharing first place for rejection were modern biblical scholarship and Charles Darwin's theory of evolution.

While biblical scholarship and evolutionary science appear to be quite different, in fact, each challenged the "history" revealed in the Bible. This posed a serious problem for fundamentalists. For them, the past is the history of salvation. Salvation history is a story, one starting with the first man, Adam, then moving to the father of the nation of Israel, Abraham, then to the mediator of God's liberation of the Hebrews from slavery, Moses, on up to the culmination of the story with Jesus, the expression of God's own self-communication. Evolutionary science produced a story, too, one of emergence and change, from a single-celled entity, dinosaur fossils, apes, and other kinds of evidence. From the sciences, fundamentalists were confronted with an earth billions of years old, not the six or ten thousand years they inferred from the Bible. The stories of salvation and science were irreconcilable.

Fundamentalists first criticized Darwin's theory of evolution as an insufficient account of origins. Although they may have difficulties acknowledging the fact of evolution, the reality of change over time, it is the method of scientific knowing itself that is of paramount concern. As its first principle, modern empirical science requires that natural explanations be given for natural phenomena. A natural explanation can be tested and verified; a supernatural explanation cannot. Accordingly, scientists "bracket God" in scientific explanation. This methodological principle is impossible for fundamentalists to accept. To them scientific method sounds suspiciously like atheism. How could the *origin* of the world be explained without God? The distinction made by scientists that they are not investigating the origin of *life* but the origin of the world and its development is a subtlety missed by conservatives. To be fair, some scientists are not fully cognizant of the distinction either. Even if the Big Bang is the "first moment" and the "originating event" of the universe, it is so as the origin of development, not being.

In contrast to the scientific account of an evolutionary universe, fundamentalists continued to insist that Genesis 1 be accepted as the revelation of *special creation*. They argue that God intervenes in nature to create each species, that species did not develop such intricate designs through chance, and that creation is revealed through Genesis 1. In this light, evolution and creation are opposing accounts of the development of the natural world. They cannot both be true. They require a choice between them.

Special creation is not a view that is intrinsic to Christian belief, nor is it common to the faith of the early church. There is a diversity among the early church theologians in their views of creation as well as their interpretations of the Genesis accounts. In his work finished in 415 C.E., *On the Literal Meaning of Genesis: A Commentary in Twelve Books*, for example, Augustine dismissed the idea that God actually created in the six days depicted in the Genesis narrative.[5] Rather, God creates everything simultaneously, in

5. Augustine, 1:154–62.

a single act, including time. Genesis 1 is to be taken meta-phorically, not as literal history.

CREATIONISM

Fundamentalists have rejected many aspects of modernity, modern science, and modern biblical scholarship; but they have not formed a separatist community. If anything, the movement has been a very public one with a political agenda. Creationists in particular have opposed evolutionary science by trying to eliminate the teaching of evolution in public schools or trying to integrate the biblical story of creation into the science classroom as an alternative to evolution.

Over the course of the twentieth century, creationists changed their self-designation as well as their strategy. The term *creation science* replaced *creationism*. In turn, *Intelligent Design* replaced *creation science*. A further term, *critical analysis*, has been introduced but has not yet taken on a life of its own. There are slight differences in approach from one designation to the other, but the reason for the changes is solely pragmatic. When courts ruled that the conduct of creationists—in posting disclaimers, and so forth—was unconstitutional, creationists changed their name in order to continue the work but avoid the judgment. The term *Intelligent Design* was introduced after the U.S. Supreme Court ruled in the 1987 case, *Edwards v. Aguillard*, that teaching creation science in public schools was unconstitutional.

Creationists have tried various means to get people to accept the Genesis story—not only as true but also as evidence against evolutionary theory. As noted above, by "creation" fundamentalists mean special creation, the creation of all life forms essentially as they are today. They take this seriously. Ronald L. Numbers describes fundamentalists home-schooling. "At Christian Liberty Academy in Arlington Heights, Illinois, for example, some 500 students learn that belief in creationism is essential not only for living in a morally acceptable manner but for achieving eternal life as well."[6] There are 30,000 students in the extended program.

The political aim of creationism is the elimination of "Darwinism." From the start they have focused on the one place where everyone will meet evolution: the high school science classroom. Thus their attention to local and state school boards and state legislators in their role as overseers of the state's educational system.

Creationist strategies have varied. The most extreme proposal advanced—and accepted in the short-term—has been to take the concept of evolution out of states' guidelines for science altogether. Failing that, they have put disclaimers in biology textbooks disputing evolution and mandated that teachers read prepared statements to the effect that evolutionary theory is flawed in some respect. Evolution is "just a theory." Theory is portrayed in common sense terms as a guess or opinion. Because the fossil record does not contain evidence of every single step in the transformation of species or the emergence of new species, they portray the "gaps" in the record as evidence that evolutionary theory is flawed. Debates and differences among scientists are signs that the theory is "falling apart." The consequences of teaching evolution, they argue, have been the breakdown of traditional values and moral behavior. They assign even the spread of

6. Numbers, "Creation Science," May 25, 1995.

HIV/AIDS to "Darwinism," their diminutive for evolutionary theory.

Creationists have also portrayed the Genesis story as a theory and advocated the inclusion of "creation science" alongside "evolutionary science" as an alternative theory. They call for science teachers to "teach the controversy," although the controversy is only at their initiation.

Religious conservatives worked hard during the first half of the twentieth century to keep publishers from treating evolution in science textbooks. When publishers did include it, creationists poured their energy into casting doubt on it. Using the strategies described above, they persuaded local school boards, state education boards, and state legislatures to restrict schools from teaching evolution. They tried to change the definition of science in state guidelines by severing the word *natural* from *explanation* in defining science, thereby leaving the way open for supernatural explanation.

Although successful with school boards and with state laws, creationists have failed in the courts. In case after case brought before courts in the last forty years or so, the courts have rebuffed creationist strategies. Courts have consistently ruled that their actions are a political violation of the First Amendment, the separation of church and state, and the Amendment's Establishment Clause, which restricts the government from favoring the religious beliefs of some over those of others. It is this restriction that fundamentalists want lifted for their particular understanding of the Earth's origins. They want a local school board or the formulation of state education requirements to mandate the inclusion of the biblical story of creation as they interpret it or to exclude the concept of evolution because it conflicts with their understanding of the way things have come into being.

INTELLIGENT DESIGN

Leaders of the Intelligent Design (ID) movement constitute a relatively small group. The names of four come up often. All are associated with the Center for Science and Culture, the ID component of the Discovery Institute, in Seattle, Washington:

- Philip Johnson is credited with starting the ID movement. He is professor of law at Boadt Hall, the University of California at Berkeley, and author of *Darwin on Trial.*

- Michael J. Behe is a biochemist and author of *Darwin's Black Box: The Biochemical Challenge to Evolution.*

- William A. Dembski, author of *The Design Inference,* is a mathematician and philosopher.

- Jonathan Wells is a molecular biologist with a doctorate in religious studies. He is author of *Icons of Evolution: Why Much of What We Teach about Evolution Is Wrong.*

As a further reframing of creationism, ID is not new. It is William Paley's *Natural Theology* revived with a mix of evolutionary biology unknown to Paley. But under the ID name biblical references disappear. The seven-day creation story, the garden, the sin of Adam and Eve, Noah, the ark, and the great flood—all these disappear. ID integrates some aspects of evolutionary theory. Its adherents present ID as a theoretical alternative. ID contrasts Darwin's mechanism for evolution, natural selection, with a different mechanism.

Identifying a *mechanism* of evolution is an answer to the question, "What accounts for the obvious complexity and diversity in the world?" Creationists reject the idea that the constellation of features in complex entities could develop through the natural process of random genetic variation. The biochemist Michael Behe argues that specific life forms are "irreducibly complex" and could not have resulted from natural selection. A cell would be an example of a irreducibly complex form. It is impossible, in his view, that such a complex entity could be produced by small successive modifications.

Behe argues that such complexity can only be explained by the direct intervention of a designer, not by a natural process. The ID argument is simple and familiar: design implies a designer. Design as intricate as the human eye—William Paley's original example—must be the result of intervention in nature by an Intelligent Designer. Behe extends this argument by offering examples on the molecular level. This Intelligent Designer is not explicitly identified with the Christian God, but the association can hardly be missed.[7]

THE RESPONSE OF SCIENTISTS

Scientists distinguish between the claim that we are presently unable to explain something (an epistemological claim) and

---

7. Helpful explanations and critiques of creationism are: Alters and Alters, *Defending Evolution*; Pennock, ed., *Intelligent Design Creationism and Its Critics*; and Pigliucci, *Denying Evolution*.

the claim that we cannot explain something and must invoke a supernatural cause (a metaphysical claim).

The epistemological claim does not cause any problems. Scientists readily concur that we are unable at the present time to explain many things. Human understanding is always incomplete. Further questions keep scientific knowing "on the move" and ever-expanding.

The metaphysical claim that we must evoke a supernatural explanation for things we cannot explain does cause problems. The physical world is not arbitrary. To put it in terms of being, there are not some physical things that develop naturally and some whose existence requires supernatural intervention. Or to put it in terms of knowing, there are not some physical things that are intelligible and can be known and others that are beyond intelligibility and require a supernatural explanation.

Scientists presume intelligibility. The natural world can be known. What we do not know awaits the right questions to generate insights that grasp just what is there to be grasped. Once the insights occur and the subsequent judgments are verified, the unknown becomes the known. What Behe calls "irreducibly complex" are admittedly complex phenomena. But they are part of the incredibly complex yet intelligible world, not instances of things created by supernatural intervention and excluded from our capacity to understand.

ID adherents portray their program as scientific. But in the judgment of evolutionary scientists, ID is a new version of an old "God of the gaps" argument in which one evokes the divine to explain phenomena not currently understood. The problem with any form of the "God of the gaps" argument is simple. When scientists *do* figure out the natural cause of whatever has been attributed to divine intervention, the need for God is eliminated. Creationists portray ID as an alternative theory to evolutionary theory. But scientists' critique of them is that they misrepresent scientific facts, have serious conceptual flaws in their formulations, and lack credible scientific evidence for their own proposals.

Scientists and philosophers of science highlight several reasons to withhold the designation "science" from the work of those committed to ID principles.

Scientific method. The first reason regards scientific method. Science is understanding. It results from raising questions, engaging in observation and experimentation, and formulating insights into the data into hypotheses. ID publications are more often critiques of evolutionary theory than reports of results from engagement with scientific method. They have been accused of misrepresenting the theory of evolution or diminishing it by referring to it as "just a theory." (Of course, gravity is "just a theory," too.) Their appeal to "teach the controversy" appears bold, but there is no controversy on the side of scientists.

Scientific concepts. A second reason regards scientific concepts. Published ID materials are often devoid of scientific content. ID advocates are not engaged primarily in scientific research. They do not have work going forward that will, in time, contribute to the advance of scientific knowledge. What concepts have been proposed have drawn direct criticism. For example, scientists do not find the concept of "irreducible complexity" persuasive and have contradicted it by tracing the pathways by which organisms and specific features of organisms develop and change.

Scientific theory. A third reason why ID is not science centers on the character of scientific theory. Appeal to a supernatural reality as the explanation of evolution or complexity cannot be tested. It fails, then, to meet a primary criterion for scientific method. Scientific knowledge results from explaining natural phenomena by their natural causes. In contrast, the ID account explains natural change by the intervention of a transcendent reality.

It would be hard for creationists to produce genuinely scientific results when they reject the methodology of modern science. Trained in graduate programs as mathematicians or scientists, creationists such as Behe, Dembski, and Fell were obviously drawn to theoretical inquiry and had the personal skills to achieve doctorates in highly technical areas. Yet their appropriation of creationism demonstrates a blind spot regarding the nature of theory and the kind of intellectual activity in which contemporary scientists are engaged.

Creationists reject the neutrality that modern science adopts by its restriction of explanations to natural causes and exclusion of any appeal to the supernatural. They see this discipline as a deliberate rejection of God rather than as a methodological means of limiting explanations to what is testable and verifiable. While religious believers promote such appeal to God, it ends up being harmful to religious belief. If God is named the cause of what is scientifically unknown, when the unknown eventually becomes known, God becomes unnecessary.

Here, reference to a prior philosophical framework may prove helpful. In naming the supernatural as the cause of natural events, creationists confuse what Thomas Aquinas distinguished as primary and secondary causality. Secondary causality refers to the finite system of laws governing the universe. Secondary causality is created. It is the condition for the possibility of the verifiable explanations that contribute cumulatively to our knowledge of reality and that serve as the ground for further prediction and experimentation. Primary causality refers to the ultimate source for secondary causality, to God as the source of the whole, to the ultimate source for the existence of the universe and its intelligibility. Primary causality is infinite, not finite. As the primary cause, God operates not by "making things" or species but as the ground of being itself.

Scientists and religious conservatives go their separate ways not just on what they know, but more fundamentally on how they know and, perhaps most significantly, the very value of knowing itself. Understanding how knowledge figures into this conflict is a major part of grasping the nature of the conflict. But ultimately, the issue is the common good. The concept of evolution is not an incidental or arbitrary concept but a foundational and necessary one for understanding the world in which we live. The world without it is not the real world, the one in which progress and the common good are contingent on meeting problems intelligently and responsibly.

THE OPINION OF COURTS

The first trial pitting science and religion against one another was the famous Scopes trial in 1925.[8] The state of Tennessee had passed House Bill 185 prohibiting evolution from being taught in the state's schools. Of itself this restriction would not

8. See Linders, "Tennessee *vs.* John Scopes."

be a violation of the separation of church and state protected by the First Amendment. The violation was appealing to the Bible as the reason for removal of evolution. The prohibition read:

> Section 1. *Be it enacted by the General Assembly of the State of Tennessee*, That it shall be unlawful for any teacher in any of the Universities, Normals and all other public schools of the State which are supported in whole or in part by the public school funds of the State, to teach any theory that denies the story of the Divine Creation of man as taught in the Bible, and to teach instead that man has descended from a lower order of animals.
>
> . . . .
>
> Section 2. *Be it further enacted*, That any teacher found guilty of the violation of this Act, Shall be guilty of a misdemeanor and upon conviction, shall be fined not less than One Hundred $100.00 Dollars nor more than Five Hundred ($500.00) Dollars for each offense.

The anti-evolution crusade was led by William Jennings Bryan, a famous attorney and several-times candidate for President. Bryan had been influential in fundamentalist efforts to legislate prohibitions against teaching evolution in fifteen states. The American Civil Liberties Union offered its services to anyone who would challenge the Tennessee law. A biology teacher in the Tennessee school system, John Scopes, agreed to do so.

The defense attorney was Clarence Darrow, a well-known lawyer like Bryan. The defense goal focused not so much on the immediate outcome of this trial—Scopes's acquittal—as the use of the case later by a higher court in having these state laws prohibiting evolution ruled unconstitutional.

In fact Scopes was not acquitted. He was found guilty and fined. And when the case went to the Tennessee Supreme Court the next year, the decision of this lower court was dismissed on a technicality. What the defense had hoped to gain was not achieved. But in a roundabout way, the fundamentalist cause was undermined. In defending scriptural inerrancy, William Jennings Bryan came off looking like a fool. Of the fifteen states considering similar anti-evolution legislation, only Arkansas and Mississippi went ahead with it at that time.

The Scopes trial received worldwide attention. On the other side of the globe, New Zealanders were kept up-to-date with the trial through newspaper articles in the secular press with titles such as "Tennessee's heresy hunt: the 'down with evolution' comedy" (*New Zealand Free Lance,* July 15, 1925). Ronald Numbers and John Stenhouse write that:

> The *New Zealand Free Lance*, a popular illus-
> trated weekly, described the event as "the most
> amazing trial held since the days of the Spanish
> Inquisition, or, say, the witchcraft 'smelling-out'
> era in Massachusetts": The prosecution of Scopes
> shows "America's freak laws at their zenith of sil-
> liness" and provided the world with "the joke of
> the decade." The day after the trial began, the New
> Zealand Herald ran a front-page story captioned
> "A crusade of darkness: blind fanaticism." Linking
> the trial to religious dogmatism and southern
> racism, the newspaper found it "hard to take the
> anti-evolution movement seriously." Such rhetoric
> established the public image of antievolutionists as

benighted fools, indigenous to the southern United States.[9]

Subsequent cases have exhibited increasing clarity and sophistication by American courts about the issues at stake and the character of the creationist ploy. In suits filed both against them and by them, courts routinely rule against creationists. The following five cases are often cited as the most important.[10]

In the 1968 case, *Epperson v. Arkansas*, the United States Supreme Court invalidated an Arkansas statute that prohibited the teaching of evolution because its primary purpose was religious, thus violating the Establishment Clause. The brief opens by summarizing the case:

> Appellant Epperson, an Arkansas public school teacher, brought this action for declaratory and injunctive relief challenging the constitutionality of Arkansas' "anti-evolution" statute. That statute makes it unlawful for a teacher in any state-supported school or university to teach or to use a textbook that teaches "that mankind ascended or descended from a lower order of animals." The State Chancery Court held the statute an abridgment of free speech violating the First and Fourteenth Amendments. The State Supreme Court, expressing no opinion as to whether the statute prohibits "explanation" of the theory or only teaching that the theory is true, reversed the Chancery Court. In a two-sentence opinion it sustained the statute as within the State's power to specify the public

9. Numbers and Stenhouse, "Antievolutionism in the Antipodes."

10. See Matsumura and Mead, "10 Significant Court Decisions Regarding Evolution/Creationism."

school curriculum. Held: The statute violates the
Fourteenth Amendment, which embraces the First
Amendment's prohibition of state laws respecting
an establishment of religion.[11]

By the 1980s, fundamentalists had adopted the language
of "creation-science" for their interpretation of the Bible.
Arkansas Act 590, titled "Balanced Treatment for Creation-
Science and Evolution-Science Act," was signed into law in
1981. The title of the act and the mandate were the same:
"Public schools within this State shall give balanced treatment
to creation-science and to evolution-science." In *McLean v.
Arkansas Board of Education* (1982), a federal court held that
this "balanced treatment" statute violated the Establishment
Clause of the U.S. Constitution.

In a 1994 California case, a high school biology teacher,
John Peloza, sued his school district for requiring him to
teach evolution against his religious beliefs and barring him
from talking to students about his religious beliefs. In *Peloza
v. Capistrano School District*, the U.S. Court of Appeals, Ninth
Circuit, upheld a district court finding that a teacher's First
Amendment right to free exercise of religion was not violated
by a school district's requirement that evolution be taught in
biology classes.

In 1994, the Tangipahoa, Louisiana, school board ap-
proved a statement asserting that the study of evolution was
"not intended to influence or dissuade the Biblical version of
Creation or any other concept." Further, it is the "basic right
and privilege of each student to form his/her own opinion
or maintain beliefs taught by parents on this very important

11. *Epperson v. Arkansas*, 393, U.S. 97 (1968).

matter of the origin of life and matter."[12] The Louisiana ACLU sued the school board, citing the disclaimer as a violation of the separation of church and state.

On appeal, in 1997, in *Freiler v. Tangipahoa Parish Board of Education*, the United States District Court for the Eastern District of Louisiana rejected this disclaimer, noting that the school board portrayed evolution as a religious viewpoint that runs counter to other religious viewpoints. This decision is also important for noting that proposals for "intelligent design," a new term, were equivalent to proposals for teaching "creation science."

The U.S. Fifth Circuit Court of Appeals agreed with the district court decision that the statement violated the First Amendment separation of church and state. These decisions, however, did not stop fundamentalists in Louisiana from trying to approve disclaimers—used in Alabama since 1996—like the one above. A December 13, 2002, *New York Times* article noted that the state's education board had rejected such a proposal at its December 12 meeting. One board member in favor of the disclaimer opposed evolution by saying, "I don't believe I evolved from some primate."

In 2005, in *Tammy Kitzmiller et al. v. Dover School District et al.*, a federal judge, John E. Jones III, offered perhaps the most thorough and sophisticated judicial assessment of the creationist/ID cause and the philosophical, scientific, and constitutional issues it raised. He ruled that the school board's 1994 requirement that teachers read a statement noting "gaps in evolutionary theory" and mandating discussion

12. Brief for *Freiler v. Tangipahoa Parish Board of Education*. Online: http://caselaw.lp.findlaw.com/scripts/getcase.pl?navby=search&case=/ data2/circs/5th/9830132cv1.html.

about "Intelligent Design" prior to discussion of evolution in class was unconstitutional. Jones identified Intelligent Design as a religious viewpoint that advances a particular version of Christianity.

Taking up the question of what constitutes science, Judge Jones emphasized that ID is not science. By appealing to a supernatural explanation, ID violates the method of modern empirical science. He cited its "dualism," whereby evidence discrediting evolution is taken as a confirmation of ID. The argument regarding "irreducible complexity," Jones wrote, is a negative argument against evolution, not proof of design.

Scientific experts, among them Francisco Ayala, a University of California biologist and philosopher of science, testified that evolutionary theory does not contradict belief in a divine creator. Judge Jones ruled that the disclaimer statement was a constitutional violation of the Establishment Clause. Because ID is not a science, he wrote in his opinion for the trial, its only purpose is the advancement of religion.

The school board members were severely criticized for blindly adopting the proposal of ID adherents while dismissing the views of science teachers and experts in the field. Judge Jones cited the "striking ignorance" of the ID concept by board members. They were quite aware that they were trying to "inject some form of creationism" into science classrooms, however. In a particularly damning judgment, Judge Jones wrote, "Any asserted secular purposes of the board are a sham and are merely secondary to a religious objective." He noted the "breathtaking inanity" of the board members' actions judged against the factual backdrop revealed by the trial.

CREATIONISM AND THE SCIENTIFIC COMMUNITY

Creationism has also challenged the scientific community to greater clarity about evolution, science, and science education. Individual scientists, professional organizations, and law courts concur overwhelmingly in the judgment that creationism under any name does not belong in science classrooms in the American public school system. For scientists, creationism violates the integrity of scientific knowledge. For the courts, creationism violates the constitutional separation of church and state. For both, the duplicity of creationists in pretending to be scientific or do science is a particular problem. Dozens of professional scientific organizations have made statements to this effect over the last decade or so.[13] Their statements offer compact summaries of the importance of evolutionary theory across the board in the sciences. The positions of the American Chemical Society and the Association for the Advancement of Science are two good examples. The statement of the former is quoted in full:

> The American Chemical Society (ACS) strongly supports the inclusion of evolution in K–12 science curricula, at an age-appropriate level, because evolution is central to our modern understanding of science. Evolutionary theory is not a hypothesis, but is the scientifically accepted explanation for the origin of species, and explains significant observations in chemistry, biology, geology, and other disciplines. Because of the overwhelming evidence supporting evolution, it has been recognized and endorsed as a key component of science

13. National Center for Science Education, "Statements from Scientific and Scholarly Organizations."

education by all major scientific societies including the National Academy of Sciences (NAS), the American Association for the Advancement of Science (AAAS), and the National Science Teachers Association (NSTA). The ACS joins these prestigious organizations in recognizing the critical importance of the scientific principles embodied in evolutionary theory.

Science is a human activity that uses the observation of natural phenomena and systems, and the study of modifications to these systems, to develop models that explain the order and function of the universe. The theory of biological evolution is based on hundreds of years of scientific observation and experimentation and tens of thousands of scientific publications. It provides students with a unifying concept that explains the incredibly rich diversity of living things and their capacity to change and evolve over time to adapt to changing environments. It is a central component of modern biology and biotechnology. Evolution is an active field of research in which new discoveries continue to increase our knowledge and understanding of the specific processes and paths that biological evolution has followed over the millions of years that life has existed on earth.

Evolution cannot be dismissed or diminished by characterizing it as mere conjecture or speculation. Scientific explanations of the natural world have been reached through observation and experimentation, are testable through observation and manipulation of natural systems, and can be modified as a result of new information. The inclusion of non-scientific explanations in science curricula misrepresents the nature and processes of science and compromises a central purpose of public education—the preparation of a scientifically literate workforce.

An early statement of the American Association for the Advancement of Science and its Commission on Science Education (1972) is notable for its clarity. During the past century and a half, the earth's crust and the fossils preserved in it have been intensively studied by geologists and paleontologists. Biologists have intensively studied the origin, structure, physiology, and genetics of living organisms. The conclusion of these studies is that the living species of animals and plants have evolved from different species that lived in the past. The scientists involved in these studies have built up the body of knowledge known as the biological theory of the origin and evolution of life. There is no currently acceptable alternative scientific theory to explain the phenomena.

The various accounts of creation that are part of the religious heritage of many people are not scientific statements or theories. They are statements that one may choose to believe, but if he does, this is a matter of faith, because such statements are not subject to study or verification by the procedures of science. A scientific statement must be capable of test by observation and experiment. It is acceptable only if, after repeated testing, it is found to account satisfactorily for the phenomena to which it is applied.

In 2002, thirty years later, the same society passed this resolution:

Recognizing that the "intelligent design theory" represents a challenge to the quality of science education, the Board of Directors of the AAAS unanimously adopts the following resolution:

Whereas, ID proponents claim that contemporary evolutionary theory is incapable of explaining the origin of the diversity of living organisms;

Whereas, to date, the ID movement has failed to offer credible scientific evidence to support their claim that ID undermines the current scientifically accepted theory of evolution;

Whereas, the ID movement has not proposed a scientific means of testing its claims;

Therefore Be It Resolved, that the lack of scientific warrant for so-called "intelligent design theory" makes it improper to include as a part of science education;

Therefore Be Further It Resolved, that AAAS urges citizens across the nation to oppose the establishment of policies that would permit the teaching of "intelligent design theory" as a part of the science curricula of the public schools . . .

THE COURT OF PUBLIC OPINION

Americans are predisposed toward taking the word of scientists as authoritative. Students will often assign "truth" to scientific statements and "opinion" to non-scientific statements. The burden of proof is on the non-scientific. In popular usage, "to know" is to know scientifically. Except in the case of evolution.

When it comes to evolution, we see a strange and muddled picture. On the one hand, Americans are unquestionably proud of their scientific and technological prowess in the world. Many work in technological fields. Complex scientific research results in new medicines and cures for once-feared diseases. Americans value scientists and science. On the other hand, they devalue and dismiss evolution as "just a theory." Confusing the meaning of both fact and theory, they describe evolutionary theory "as just a theory and not a fact." Scientists are no longer authoritative voices when it comes to the development of the universe, although, from the viewpoint of scientists themselves, the evidence for evolution is overwhelming.

Several polls taken over the last several years confirm this fact: many Americans have not integrated scientific views about evolution into their personal understanding of the world.[14] A poll taken in August 2006 by the Pew Forum on Religion and Public Policy found that 42 percent of those polled agreed with the statement that God created human beings essentially as they are today about 10,000 years ago. Slightly more people, 48 percent, believed that human beings had evolved. But 65 percent of white evangelicals polled believe that humans have existed only in their present form. Among those who accept evolution, the Pew poll found that 21 percent thought that evolutionary changes were guided directly by a supreme being. Only 26 percent believed that evolution was due to natural selection, as Darwin and subsequent scientists have argued. A strong majority of those

14. University of California Museum on Paleontology, "Understanding Evolution"; The Pew Forum on Religion and Public Life 2005 survey, "Public Divided on Origins of Life"; Harris Interactive Inc. 2005 survey, "Nearly Two-thirds of U.S. Adults Believe Human Beings Were Created by God."

polled, 64 percent, thought that both creation and evolution should be taught in schools. And 38 percent agreed with the statement that *only* creationism should be taught. The Gallop and Harris polls have had similar results.

Such results are alarming because they indicate the extent to which creationists have affected all of public opinion. The power of fundamentalist creationists to set the terms of this debate far outweighs their numerical percentage within Christian denominations. Many people who would not identify themselves at all with creationism describe their own views in terms that are virtually identical to the way creationists formulate the issues, affirming, for example, that:

- Evolutionary theory leads to atheism. *FALSE*

- Creation means God's created things in six days.

- Creation and evolution are opposing accounts of "what happened." *FALSE*

- Creation gives purpose and meaning to the world.

- Evolution is random and directionless. *FALSE*

- It is only fair that both sides or both theories be presented. *FALSE - not in a science class*

- A theory is not quite as good as a fact. *"Just a theory"*

- No one was there; we can't say what happened.

Thus, despite the continual efforts of mainline churches, state and federal courts, and eminent scientific guilds, many if not most Americans subscribe to a major misunderstanding of our evolutionary world, the scientific enterprise, and what it means to affirm God as "creator of heaven and earth."

a theory is supported by a large amount of empirical evidence

STUDENT MISUNDERSTANDINGS

Similar misunderstanding is evident among American college students. None of the students quoted below are identified with creationism. But their student essays showed an understanding of the issue shaped almost exclusively by the creationist views. Even to refer to the "conflict between creation and evolution" is an indication of this influence. Students often have little with which to counter easy positions picked up from the public airing of fundamentalist views. Their understanding of scientific method and what makes science is often weak. Their conception of evolution rarely reflects a scientific grasp of what scientists consider the unifying concept of the sciences.

Both creationists and evolutionary scientists, for example, speak of the *theory* of creation in Genesis, the latter to embrace it, the former to reject it. Both conceive of *creation* without reference to its technical meaning in the theological tradition. Students are often indifferent to which "theory" is right—creation or evolution. They await proof. This student writes:

> Most of the people making decisions about creation *v.* evolution are more concerned about the separation between church and state rather than the truth (no matter what that may be). Evolution is a theory and Intelligent Design comes from the Bible but neither one have been proven fact. Intelligent Design is not allowed in science classrooms but the theory of evolution is. Each side should be given a fair chance in schools until one has been proved fact. It comes down to open-mindedness. Most Americans chose only to believe what they want to and are not open to hearing other people's

> opinions no matter how right or wrong. Atheists don't want to believe. You could prove beyond all doubt that Intelligent Design exists and these people would deny it forever. It is in our nature to question everything and whether or not Intelligent Design exists or not, I don't know but I believe that believers should be allowed to research it and it should be allowed to be taught in our schools.

Creationists often portray evolutionary theory as one step away from disintegration. They portray what scientists do not yet understand as "gaps" or deficiencies in the theory. One student wrote that "because evolution is just a theory, there are many holes in it that are unexplainable at this time," an almost-verbatim criticism found in creationists' writings.

The creationists' disparagement of evolution as "just a theory" suggests there is something wrong with theory or that one comes down from something to theory. Theories are dismissed. What this student says is voiced by students routinely:

> Evolution is at heart, a theory, not something gained on hard data. There are gaps in this theory that the scientist fills with things of material origins. Empirical data can be misinterpreted, and no one was there at the beginning, which makes all this conjecture. Evolution is opposed to the Bible. One has a creation of six days; the other is a random set of things. Religion and science contradict one another in this and other issues.

Especially obvious is the creationists' equivalence of Genesis 1 and creation, which then makes creation and evolution opposites. They are two mutually contradictory accounts of what happened. This student writes:

> The Bible is involved in the debate over creation and evolution because the Bible claims that God is the one creator of all living things. The debate is over whether all things were created by God or they have come to be over a long period of time. Science and religion cannot agree on this. Moreover, some things are too complicated to have simply evolved. They must have been created by God.

The creationist view that evolutionary theory leads to conflict between evolution and creation also shows up in student thinking. This student writes:

> Evolution is the answer for people who don't have faith in a spirit world and who believe that the world is completely due to scientific processes. Evolution is a process in which the world was created by "random atomic collisions." The Bible describes creation occurring over six days. God describes each creation as "good" which describes the importance and value of each creation. Evolution describes things coming to be at "random" implying that this process was perhaps a mistake. The process by which the world was created has been a topic of debate for many years. The issue is whether the process was scientific or the work of God. Were human beings formed by evolution from previous animal-like creatures or by the work of God? Those who believe in God believe the process in the creation story is the sole reason the world and people exist.

Many presume that this conflict is unavoidable. Whatever debate takes place on the issue is formulated in creationists' terms.

SIX

Fundamentalist Anxiety

While the Intelligent Design movement downplays the Genesis 1 creation story in its public challenges to evolutionary theory, the historicity of the creation story remains as important personally to the individuals involved as it was under its other names. Pressed, they would defend special creation over against evolution just as creationists and creation scientists would have done.

Yet even when we acknowledge that the historicity of Genesis 1 is so important to religious conservatives, that is, Genesis 1 as fact, this does not tell us *why* it is so important to them. With such compelling evidence to the contrary, what makes this such a crucial position to defend? For answers most turn to the obvious, the biblical literalism of fundamentalism. Literalism and historicity go hand in hand. The implicit fundamentalist epistemology—their assumed theory of knowledge—makes *truth* largely equivalent to *history*. If x is historical, it is true. If y is true, it is historical. Truth is the positive answer to the question, "Did this happen?" To be true, Genesis 1 must be the account of a historical event.

Although clarifying, this explanation remains incomplete. While it may capture the narrow notion of truth that biblical literalists share, it does not explain their anxiety.

Their insistence that Genesis 1 must be historical to be true is not shared by all Christians, to be sure. Many people have a notion of truth in which the symbolic as well as the historical convey what is true. Many have gradually replaced their literal reading of the biblical story as a child with a symbolic reading of the story as an adult without losing God in the transition. It is more the case that losing belief in God occurs precisely because this transition has not been made. Faith is vulnerable in an adult believer with childhood beliefs. Moreover, it is not the case that belief in God as Creator and belief in Genesis 1 as symbolic are mutually exclusive. At the least, to hold divine creation in tension with an evolving universe is not impossible for believers.

But the fundamentalist "defense against all reason" is an anxious one. There is more than their method of biblical interpretation at work and at stake. The chief reason is the concept of sin and its remedy.

For fundamentalists, the special creation revealed in Genesis 1 is only a prelude to the real issue for their faith. What God created good, human beings distorted through sin. Early Christian theologians grounded the necessity for Christ's redemptive death in Genesis 3. Because of Adam's sin, all humanity is sinful, all are in need of reconciliation with God. In explaining the universality of sin by way of an *inherited* sin—the meaning of original sin—Christian theologians made Adam's sin the reason for the Incarnation and the cause of Christ's coming. Both the meaning of Christ as well as the meaning and indispensability of the church—its *chris-*

tology and *ecclesiology*—became a function of the doctrine of original sin.[1]

The catechetical exchange of question and answer is familiar: *Why did Christ come? To reconcile humankind with God. Why is reconciliation necessary? Because all have the sin of Adam and Eve.* What happens to Christ if Adam and Eve are not historical? This is the question that drives fundamentalist anxiety.

The fundamentalist crisis created by modernity is primarily christological. With their presupposition of the inerrancy of the Bible and an epistemology that links truth with historicity, fundamentalists have created a set of building blocks ready to fall if any of them is removed. The chief structural blocks are these:

- if the Bible presents God creating the universe in this way, then God must have done so or the Bible is not true;

- if the Bible presents Adam and Eve as historical persons, then they must be historical or the Bible is not true;

- if the Bible presents the sin of Adam and Eve as the first sin, then it must be historical or the Bible is not true;

- if the Bible presents the obedience of Christ as an answer to the disobedience of Adam, then both must be historical or the Bible is not true.

1. On the development of this doctrine, see Wiley, *Original Sin.*

Their crisis could be put this way:

- without the historicity of creation, there is no historical Adam or sin;

- without the historicity of Adam's sin, there is no
  reason for Christ;

- without a reason for Christ, there is no redemption;

- without redemption, there is no reason for faith or
  for Christianity.

The crisis projected by fundamentalists is real enough. Adam and Eve, in fact, have disappeared from history. In the story of the past as constructed by modern scientists, there is no garden, no single couple, no first sin. In the analysis of the biblical text in modern biblical scholarship, the garden, the couple, and the first sin exist within the world of narrative, not in the world of history.

The response of fundamentalists has been to protect the master narrative at the cost of rejecting the actual world we inhabit and discover. It is for this reason that fundamentalists tell their children that belief in *creationism* is necessary for salvation.[2] It is not difficult to find evidence of this fear of the

2. For those growing up in a conservative tradition, the contradiction between their religious beliefs and what they learn in school is acute. An acquaintance writes to me in a personal note: "As a young child, growing up as One of Jehovah's Witness I learned that that each 'day' in Genesis chapter 1 represents 7000 years. The Earth is 42,000 years old. The Earth, then, is much younger than what scientists say. In second grade they taught us that the earth had been around for millions of years, that there had been species like the dinosaurs who had lived millions of years ago right where my school now stood. The idea of ancient dinosaurs, of ancient species, living long ago right where my desk was, excited me. There were books that I was not supposed to read. I was told

domino effect and the christological anxiety it produces. The relation between original sin and Christ is clear in this first example, as is the decision that the master story be protected regardless of what we discover scientifically about the world. This fundamentalist puts the matter clearly:

> "Original Sin" is one of the core theological reasons that a Christian cannot embrace the theory of evolution. Regardless of the scientific issues that now plague the evolutionary belief system, the whole message of Christianity starts with mankind's fall from paradise into death through Adam's sin. With evolution, we envision millions and millions of years of death, decay and disease before Adam even came on the scene. However, this picture is not consistent with the "very good" earth created by God. More importantly, as one can thoroughly investigate, death before sin is theologically inconsistent with the rest of Christian doctrine. . . . The whole justification of Jesus' life and death is predicated on the existence of Adam and the forbidden fruit he and Eve ate. Without the original sin, who needs to be redeemed? Without Adam's fall into a life of constant sin terminated by death, what purpose is there to Christianity? None.[3]

This anxiety is voiced in various ways, but it is assuaged chiefly through the assertion of inerrancy, that what is presented as

that many things they taught in school were lies against Jehovah. When I got home I couldn't help but ask my mom about the dinosaur's bones and the earth being millions of years old. She told me the schools teach things that are lies against Jehovah. The next day my Mom went to meet Mrs. Finch again and I had to show them every book that came from school. I was embarrassed to look at Mrs. Finch."

3. Coppedge, "Cosmology's Error Bars."

historical must be so to be *true*. These three persons all start from that presupposition:

- If Genesis can be placed in doubt, the fall of man and the need for salvation is placed in doubt. The evolution question is not a side issue. It is central to the understanding of God's word![4]

- There is no doubt that the book of Genesis is the foundational book of Scripture . . . Once Genesis is compromised, the rest of Scripture falls to compromise.

- There is an important reason to interpret from the Bible that Adam was a real person. Unless the concept of original sin through Adam is true, Jesus' coming makes no sense. That is, Christians believe that Christ's atoning sacrifice for our sins was necessary because of man's sinful nature inherited from Adam. The Bible teaches that Jesus was the "second Adam." So if Adam was not real, thus did not bring sin into the world, Christ's redemptive sacrifice was not necessary.[5]

This particular—and problematic—constellation of historical, exegetical, and theological convictions become clear in this argument from a faculty member of Westminster Seminary in California. In an article titled, "Was Adam an Historical Person? And What Difference Does It Make?" Robert B. Strimple addressed this core dilemma. The article

4. http://www.christiananswers.net.

5. http://160.94.9.156/index2.cfm?nav=90&parent=3&type=S&content_path=../ahc_trials/&content_name=Clinical_Trials&pic=eyebank2.jpg&gif=Clinical_Trials.

makes the starting point in biblical inerrancy and history explicit: "Does the Bible present Adam as an historical person, a man who actually lived at a certain point in history, the very first man and the father of all the members of the human race who followed after him? And if so, what is the theological significance of that fact? Or, to put it another way, what would be the theological consequences of denying the historicity of Adam?[6]

Strimple begins by saying that he wants to examine the theological consequences of denying the historicity of Adam: "The question is whether there really was a first man specially created by God, morally perfect in knowledge, righteousness, and holiness, as the apostle Paul teaches us, who by his own free act, for which he alone was responsible (not God, not Satan) sinned against his Maker and brought sin and death upon all his posterity."[7]

His description of the features of this first man is drawn from the theological tradition and especially the postbiblical theological discussion of original sin rather than Paul; but the later tradition has been fused with earlier biblical voices. Strimple takes the example of several modern theologians who have denied the historicity of Adam. He then reinforces the idea that by the Fall is meant the sin of the first man. The consequences of this first sin for all are: (1) the guilt was imputed to all; (2) the punishment for this sin, death, was imputed as well; and (3) because all thoughts, words, and actions are defiled by this sin, human nature is depraved or corrupted.

6. Originally published in *Christian Renewal* in 1989.
7. Ibid.

If there was no Fall, Strimple argues, then human nature as created by God must be itself sinful. He lists the consequences as he sees them in a statement infused with urgency. We see the building blocks falling: "But, mark it well, without a doctrine of the Fall there is no hope of Redemption. There is no 'Good News'! There is no Biblical Christianity! That's what is at stake here, nothing less than that."[8]

If Adam is symbolic, Strimple says, maybe Christ is, too. But what is clear is that if there is no sin to forgive, there is no reason for Christ. The death of Christ is redemptive because it pays back the debt owed for *this* sin, Adam's sin. Strimple concludes with the dilemma created by the presuppositions about the Bible and truth with which he has started. The Bible, he says, presents Adam as historical, so: "The one who rejects the Biblical teaching regarding the historical Adam and the historical Fall will find no firm basis for accepting the Biblical teaching regarding the historical, Incarnate Redeemer."[9]

Strimple is not alone. After chastising other fundamentalists for their "capitulation to evolution" in saying that Genesis 1 was not intended to teach how God created the universe, another writer for a fundamentalist Baptist website argues on various grounds that the Genesis story should be taken literally. His conclusion, however, is not about creation or the creation story but about Christ. "If Adam and Eve were not historical figures," the author writes, "the fall is a myth and redemption through the cross of Christ is nonsense." Further, the author argues: "To deny the historicity of Adam is to deny Jesus Christ. He referred to Adam and Eve as historic (Mark 10:6–8). His genealogy is traced from Adam (Luke 3:23–38).

8. Ibid.
9. Ibid.

Further, the New Testament makes direct comparisons between Christ and Adam (Rom 5:17; 1 Cor 15:22–45)."[10]

THE CHOICE OF CERTITUDE

Determining that the fundamentalist concern is with original sin rather than with creation as such does not eliminate the problems created by their attempts to eliminate evolution in science programs. But just as the value in science is understanding, so understanding "fundamentalist anxiety" in itself is a value. Scientific consensus about the centrality of the concept of evolution will not change, nor will the dynamic character of a universe in process. But knowing one's interlocutor makes a difference.

By insisting that Christian belief be certain and unchanging, fundamentalists have created a situation in which so much has to be rejected to protect their security. In the ancient world, long before the sciences of geology and paleontology, people could think that the world was only four thousand or six thousand years old. But what we think about the world today is different. The same human intelligence that allows us to travel by air across the world has discovered ways of determining the earth's age at four billion and our galaxy's at approximately thirteen billion years. The ancient person could think of Adam and Eve as historical persons living some fixed set of generations ago. Now, thinking of human evolution over hundreds of thousands of years, we no longer even have the image of a manageable set of generations.

10. Way of Life Literature's Fundamental Baptist Information Service, "Genesis Is Literal History."

Religious certainty has to ignore historical details. Even for the ancients, Adam was considered historical in a different way than, say, Abraham or Moses or David. The historicity of Adam and Eve became more important in the Christian tradition only when the first sin was understood to be an inherited sin and thus the reason why Christ's grace of forgiveness was necessary for all.

But it is not the case that Christians understood redemption exclusively as substitutionary atonement and in relation to original sin. The theological tradition offers multiple images and reasons for the Incarnation, not just one. The necessity for Christ may be eliminated with the disappearance of Adam and Eve as historical persons, and with Christ goes the reason for Christianity itself, but *only* if one's highest value is certainty and the richness of the theological tradition ignored.

Holding the Bible as inerrant—as the source for scientific and historical truth—has to do with choosing certitude as the primary tool for overcoming the insecurities brought about by modernity. Inerrancy is certainly not intrinsic to Christian faith. In the end, it threatens the credibility of faith more than evolutionary theory could ever do. When certitude is derived from the Bible, a text thoroughly situated in a premodern and prescientific culture, the tensions between the contemporary world and religious faith are endless.

This controversy fundamentalists have created over evolution is the most visible example of tension. The attempt to make Genesis 1 an alternative theory to evolutionary theory is flawed in numerous ways, but perhaps the deepest flaw is the lack of faith that accompanies it, the refusal to admit God as Creator of the actual universe that exists. While William Paley's appeal to design and purpose as evidence for God's existence had its difficulties as an argument and is no more successful in its Intelligent Design use, still the world should not be discounted as evidence of its ultimate source. If the existence and intelligibility of the universe are grounded in divine choice, from a theological perspective we can affirm an evolutionary universe in all its complexity, randomness, chance, as that which is chosen. While the words *choice* and *chosen* may seem to make divine reality more like us than is comfortable, on the other hand, we cannot talk about the fact of intelligibility without positing divine intelligence or the fact of existence with positing divine choice. The shift from nothing to something may not require preexisting matter, but it does imply choice. But at minimum, the theological principle is clear: what exists cannot be contrary to divine intention. Evolution may be a surprise to us, but not to God.

Fundamentalists argue that evolutionary theory threatens the idea that human beings are made in the image of God. It is true that modern developments have cast suspicion on the long-standing identification of *males* with the divine image in a patriarchal social order and for gender subordination to be derived from granting men the image of God and denying it to women. Theologically, however, this idea of image of God is still meaningful. Bernard Lonergan locates it in the human capacity for self-transcendence. He writes: "To say that God created the world for his glory is to say that he created it not for his sake but for ours. He made us in his image, for our authenticity consists in being like him, in self-transcending, in being origins of value, in true love."[11]

11. Lonergan, *Method in Theology*, 116–17. The discussion here on self-transcendence and below on authenticity and unauthenticity draws from Lonergan. See the index in *Method* under these terms.

Self-transcendence is cognitional, moral, and affective. Cognitional self-transcendence occurs when we *understand*, moral self-transcendence when we *make responsible decisions*, and affective when we *love*. Persons of faith are sometimes so engrossed in religious propositions that they fail to see the significance of ordinary occurrences. Self-transcendence has cosmic significance. Our growing understanding, including the on-going, cumulative quest of science, is itself an instance of an evolving universe. Understanding, not certitude, is the means for contributing to the good of the universe. It is the way in which we collaborate with God in the divinely ordained, on-going realization of the universe.

FROM CLARIFICATION TO JUDGMENT

In the preface I identified a central task of this book as one of clarification. To see this conflict over evolution from both its theological and scientific sides, we have treated the Bible and its interpretation, the Christian theological tradition, the nature and results of sciences, and nature of fundamentalist belief and creationist activity. I have made certain judgments with regard to each.

On the Bible, I have:

- situated the origin of Genesis 1 in the distress of the sixth-century B.C.E. exile of Judeans to Babylon and their continuing hope in the goodness of creation and the power of God over evil;

- rejected the idea that Genesis 1 is a theory or intended as a revelation of the way in which the universe came to be;

- separated fundamentalist from mainline Christian traditions and identified the tendency of scientists and others to talk about the Bible and creation in fundamentalist terms as if they represented Christian belief generally.

On the theological meaning of creation, I have:

- rejected the fundamentalist equivalence of *Genesis 1* and *creation* as the meaning of creation;

- grounded the theological meaning of creation in relation to the metaphysical question, "Why is there anything at all?"

- rejected the idea that creation denotes the way things have come to be and that we have to choose between two ways, creation or evolution;

On evolutionary science, I have:

- affirmed creation and evolution as answers to different questions about the universe;

- defined theoretical understanding as a differentiation in consciousness and the source of explanatory knowledge of the world;

- defined truth as verified judgments and scientific knowing as a cumulative process of verifying hypotheses about the nature world;

- showed from both a scientific and a theological point of view why bracketing the supernatural as an explanation is legitimate and necessary to do.

On the conservative religious reaction to evolution, I have:

- connected fundamentalist rejections of modernity to the changes that modern science and history have brought to our understanding of the past;

- related fundamentalist belief in Christ's atonement to the historicity of creation, Genesis 1, and the historicity of Adam and Eve and sin, Genesis 2–3;

- uncovered the christological reasons for fundamentalist anxieties.

Ultimately the critique of creationists must include not only attention to their understanding but also to their responsibility. Do their interests serve the common good? Can taking evolution out of science programs or integrating Genesis 1 into the consideration of the world's origins and development contribute to the good?

From our minds comes the grasp of problems we face and insights into the nature of the solutions we must engage. Without commitment to theoretical understanding—to the sciences—our retreat, not just into a premodern world but a primitive one, would be rapid. Insights into evolution affect everything. It is not an incidental concept but a necessary and foundational one.

Even aside from trying to make Genesis 1 a theory—a task doomed from the beginning—there is what Bernard Lonergan calls the essentialism of this kind of thinking about creation, which he contrasts with an "open intellectualist" view.

Consider how the fundamentalist theological orientation is always in the direction of control. This controversy shows that they want to control not just human beings but God, too. They want to say how and what God can or cannot create.

By trying to eliminate evolution from schools, creationists are saying, in effect, that God *cannot* have created the world order that exists. God creates only the world order that they say exists. But faith works the other way around. In this case, we need a complete turn-around in how we think about creation. It is not that thing after thing is created and then God knows what it is like as a world order. Rather, *God knows the world order in its entirety.* This means that God *knows* the world order of our universe as dynamic, open, evolutionary and all things within this world order as having the potentialities and possibilities of finite nature in an evolutionary world. What we discover about the world, as I have suggested, God already knows, because its existence and intelligibility are reflections of God's specific choice. It is God who chooses a world order in which, in the order of being, biological evolution is the fundamental feature of the natural world and, in the order of knowing, evolution is the foundational concept of the natural sciences.[12]

ASSESSING FAITH

The study of rocks may be fascinating, but the data are not dialectical, as is human meaning. With rocks we do not have to anticipate that along with insights we will find biases, with good ideas we will find bad ones, and with worthwhile proposals we find self- and group-interested ones. Rocks have no ideas and decisions with which vested interests can interfere.

12. Lonergan, "The Natural Desire to See God," 85.

The primary battle for human beings, on the other hand, is with such interference. Our capacity for raising questions is the means for becoming authentic—truly intelligent, genuinely reasonable in judgments, and fully responsible in making choices and decisions. But this capacity is not an automatic process. Insights can be blocked if they are unwelcome, judgments can be irrational, and decisions can be short-sighted. Inauthenticity—being more or less unintelligent, irrational, and irresponsible—is easy.

Given the dialectical character of human meaning and value, we can anticipate that religious faith can be both authentic and inauthentic. To be authentic, faith must be no less than attentive, intelligent, reasonable, and responsible. At the least, religious faith should promote the good. We can raise these questions for a start:

- Is a religious faith that would truncate science programs across the nation, for their children and ours, *good*?

- Is a religious faith that takes a pre-modern and patriarchal conception of belief as normative *good*?

- Is a religious faith that is closed to the overwhelming evidence for the defining feature of the universe *good*?

- How does a faith that rejects evolution accept an ultimate reality who originates and grounds an evolving universe in all its potentialities and probibilities? Is it *good*?

- Is a faith that denies evolution capable of turning around and thinking of ourselves as co-creators in the realization of open and incomplete universe? Is it *good*?

- Are creationists engaged honestly and intelligently in scientific inquiry? Are their judgments about the physical world reasonable? Is what they ask of science teachers and school boards responsible? Are their engagement, their judgments, their demands *good*?

The answers we give to these questions constitute our evaluation of the activity and agenda of creationists today. The courts have made consistent judgments about the legal implications of the creationist agenda. Scientists are of one voice about the evidence for evolution and the viability of creationists' counter-claim. The courts and scientists agree that creationism is not science but religion. To these voices, theologians add theirs. The theology advanced by creationism is not any better than its science. The critique of theology legitimately includes the question of authenticity. On the basis of honesty and consideration for the human good alone, one would have reasons to suspect the authenticity of the faith that accompanies the creationist agenda.

Bibliography

Abbott, Walter M., editor. *The Documents of Vatican II*. Translations directed by Joseph Gallagher. New York: Herder & Herder, 1966.

Alters, B. J., and S. M. Alters. *Defending Evolution: A Guide to the Evolution/Creation Controversy*. Sudbury, MA: Jones and Bartlett, 2001.

Appleby, R. Scott. "History in the Fundamentalist Imagination." *The Journal of American History* 89 (2002) 498–511.

———, and Martin E. Marty. "Fundamentalism." *Foreign Policy* 128 (2002) 16–22.

———, and Martin E. Marty, editors. *The Fundamentalism Project*. 5 vols. Chicago: University of Chicago Press, 1991.

Aquinas, Thomas. *Summa Theologica: Latin Text and English Translation, Introductions, and Notes*. 61 vols. Cambridge: Cambridge University Press, 2006.

Arnhart, Larry. "The Truth, Goodness, and Beauty of Darwinism." *Zygon* 36 (2001) 77–92.

Augustine. *On the Literal Meaning of Genesis: A Commentary in Twelve Books*. Translated by John Raymond Taylor. New York: Newman, 1981.

Ayala, Francisco. *Darwin and Intelligent Design*. Minneapolis: Fortress, 2007.

Barr, James. *Fundamentalism*. London: SCM, 1977.

Behe, Michael J. *Darwin's Black Box: The Biochemical Challenge to Evolution*. New York: Free Press, 1996.

———, William A. Dembski, and Stephen J. Meyer. *Science and Evidence for Design in the Universe*. San Francisco: Ignatius, 2000.

Benz, Arnold. "Theology in a Dynamic Universe." *Zygon* 36 (2001) 557–62.

Bleckmann, Charles A. "Evolution and Creationism in *Science*: 1880–2000." *BioScience* 56 (2006) 151–58.

Brooke, John Hedley. "Einstein, God, and Time." *Zygon* 41 (2006) 941–83.

Byrne, Patrick H. "Evolution, Randomness, and Divine Purpose: A Reply to Cardinal Schönborn." *Theological Studies* 67 (2006) 653–65.

Carroll, William E. "Creation, Evolution, and Thomas Aquinas." *Revue des Questions Scientifiques* 171 (2000) 319–47.

Catechism of the Catholic Church. Liguori, MO: Liguori, 1994.

Center for the Renewal of Science and Culture. "The Wedge Strategy." Online: http:www.antievolution.org/features/wedg.html.

Clayton, Philip. "Emerging God: Theology of a Complex Universe." *Christian Century* 121/1 (2004) 26–30.

Cobb, John B. Jr., *Back to Darwin: A Richer Account of Evolution.* Grand Rapids: Eerdmans, 2008.

Coogan, Michael D., editor. *The New Oxford Annotated Bible with the Apocryphal/Deuterocanonical Books.* 3rd ed. Oxford: Oxford University Press, 2001.

Coppedge, David F. "Cosmology's Error Bars." Online: http://www.icr.org/index.php?module=articles&action=type&ID=1.

Darwin, Charles. *The Origin of Species by Means of Natural Selection or the Preservation of Favoured Races in the Struggle for Life.* London: Murray, 1859.

Davis, Percival, and H. Kenyon Dean. *Of Pandas and People: The Central Question of Biological Origins.* 2nd ed. Dallas: Haughton, 1993.

Dawkins, Richard. *The Blind Watchmaker: Why the Evidence of Evolution Reveals a Universe without Design.* With a new Introduction. New York: Norton, 1996.

Dayton, Donald W. "Creationism in Twentieth-Century America." *Zygon* 32 (1997) 105–13.

Dembski, William A. *The Design Inference: Eliminating Chance through Small Probabilities.* Cambridge Studies in Probability, Induction and Decision Theory. Cambridge: Cambridge University Press, 1998.

———. *Intelligent Design: The Bridge between Science and Religion.* Downers Grove, IL: InterVarsity, 1999.

———. *No Free Lunch: Why Specified Complexity Cannot Be Purchased without Intelligence.* Lanham, MD: Rowman & Littlefield, 2002.

———. *The Wedge of Truth: Splitting the Foundations of Naturalism.* Downers Grove, IL: InterVarsity, 2000.

Epperson v. Arkansas, 393, U.S. 97 (1968). Online: http://caselaw .lp.findlaw.com/scripts/getcase.pl?court=US&vol=393&invol=97.

Forrest, Barbara. "Understanding the Intelligent Design Creationist Movement: Its True Nature and Goals." Position Paper from the Center for Inquiry, Office of Public Policy. May, 2007. Online: http:// www.centerforinquiry.net/uploads/attachments/intelligent-design .pdf.

———, and Paul R. Gross. *Creationism's Trojan Horse: The Wedge of Intelligent Design.* Oxford: Oxford University Press, 2003.

Grant, Robert, and David Tracy. *A Short History of the Interpretation of the Bible.* 2nd ed. Philadelphia: Fortress, 1984.

Harris Interactive. 2005 Survey: "Nearly Two-thirds of U.S. Adults Believe Human Beings Were Created by God." Online: http:// harrisineractive.com/harris_poll/index.asp?PID=581.

Institute for Creation Science. "Introduction to ICR." Online: http://www .icr.org/abouticr/intro.htm.

Jaki, Stanley L. "The Role of Faith in Physics." *Zygon* 2 (1967) 187–202.

Jennings, William H. *Storms over Genesis: Biblical Battleground in America's Wars of Religion.* Minneapolis: Fortress, 2007.

Johnson, Philip. *Darwin on Trial.* 2nd ed. Downers Grove, IL: InterVarsity, 1993.

Haught, John F. *Christianity and Science: Toward a Theology of Nature.* Theology in Global Perspective Series. Maryknoll, NY: Orbis, 2007.

———. *God after Darwin: A Theology of Evolution.* Boulder, CO: Westview, 2000.

———. *Responses to 101 Questions on God and Evolution.* New York: Paulist, 2001.

Henig, Robin Marantz. *The Monk in the Garden: The Lost and Found Genius of Gregor Mendel, the Father of Genetics.* Boston: Houghton Mifflin, 2000.

Hodgson, Peter C. *Liberal Theology: A Radical Vision.* Minneapolis: Fortress, 2007.

International Theological Commission. "Communion and Stewardship: Human Persons Created in the Image of God." Online: http://www .bringyou.to/apologetics/p80.htm.

Kee, Howard Clark, Eric M. Meyers, John Rogerson, and Anthony J. Saldarini. *The Cambridge Companion to the Bible*. Cambridge: Cambridge University Press, 1997.

Linders, Douglas. "Tennessee vs. John Scopes: The 'Monkey Trial' 1925." Online: http://www.law.umkc.edu/faculty/projects/ftrials/scopes/ scopes.htm.

Lonergan, Bernard J. F., SJ. *Insight: A Study of Human Understanding*. London: Darton, Longman and Todd, 1957.

———. *Insight: A Study of Human Understanding*. Edited by Frederick E. Crowe and Robert M. Doran. Collected Works of Bernard Lonergan 3. Toronto: University of Toronto Press, 1992. Orig. ed., 1957.

———. *Method in Theology*. New York: Herder and Herder, 1972.

———. "The Natural Desire to See God." In *Collection: Papers by Bernard J. F. Lonergan*, edited by Frederick E. Crowe and Robert M. Doran, 81–91. Collected Works of Bernard Lonergan 4.Toronto: University of Toronto Press, 1988.

Matsumura, Molleen, and Louise Mead. "10 Significant Court Decisions Regarding Evolution/Creationism." National Center for Science Education. Online: http://www.ncseweb.org/resources/articles/ 5690_10_significant_court_decisions_2_15_2001.asp.

Mayr, Ernst. *What Evolution Is*. New York: Basic Books, 2001.

———, and Michael Ruse. *Darwin and Design: Does Evolution Have a Purpose?* Cambridge: Harvard University Press, 2003.

McCalla, Arthur. *The Creationist Debate: The Encounter between the Bible and the Historical Mind*. London: T. & T. Clark, 2006.

Miller, Kenneth. *Finding Darwin's God: A Scientist's Search for Common Ground between God and Evolution*. New York: HarperCollins, 1999.

———. *Perspectives on an Evolving Creation*. Grand Rapids: Eerdmans, 2003.

Moore, J. R. *The Post-Darwinian Controversies: A Study of the Protestant Struggle to Come to Terms with Darwin in Great Britain and America, 1870–1900*. Cambridge: Cambridge University Press, 1979.

Moore, Randy, Murray Jensen, and Jay Hatch. "Twenty Questions: What Have the Courts Said about the Teaching of Evolution and Creationism in Public Schools?" *BioScience* 53 (2003) 766–71.

Morris, Henry M. *The Long War against God: The History and Impact of the Creation/Evolution Conflict*. Grand Rapids: Baker, 1989.

———. *The Scientific Case for Creationism*. San Diego: Creation-Life, 1977.

National Academy of Science. "Evolution Resources." Online: http://nationalacademies.org/evolution/.

———. "Science, Evolution, Creationism." Online: http://www.nap.edu/catalog.php?record_id=11876.

National Center for Science Education. "Statements from Scientific and Scholarly Organizations." Online: http://www.ncseweb.org/resources/articles/8408_statements_from_scientific_and_12_19_2002.asp.

Nielsen, Niels. *Fundamentalism, Mythos and World Religions*. Albany: State University of New York Press, 1993.

Numbers, Ronald L. "Creation Science." *Christian Century* 112/18 (1995) 574–75.

———. *The Creationists*. Expanded ed. Cambridge: Harvard University Press, 2006.

Numbers, Ronald L., and Jon Stenhouse. "Antievolutionism in the Antipodes: From Protesting Evolution to Promoting Creationism in New Zealand." *The British Journal for the History of Science* 33 (2000) 335–50.

———, editors. *Disseminating Darwin: The Role of Place, Race, Religion, and Gender*. Cambridge: Cambridge University Press, 1999.

Paley, William. *Natural Theology, or, Evidences of the Existence and Attributes of the Deity, Collected from the Appearances of Nature*. Boston: Gould & Lincoln, 1860.

Pearson, Birger A. *Ancient Gnosticism: Traditions and Literature*. Minneapolis: Fortress, 2007.

Pennock, Robert. "Creationism and Intelligent Design." *Annual Review of Genomics and Human Genetics* 4 (2003) 143–63.

———, editor. *Intelligent Design Creationism and Its Critics: Philosophical, Theological, and Scientific Perspectives*. Cambridge, MA: MIT Press, 2001.

————. *Tower of Babel: The Evidence against the New Creationism.* Cambridge, MA: MIT Press, 1999.

Perkins, Pheme. *The Gnostic Dialogue: The Early Church and the Crisis of Gnosticism.* New York: Paulist, 1980.

————. *Gnosticism in the New Testament.* Minneapolis: Fortress, 1993.

Peters, Ted. "Cosmos and Creation." *Word & World* 4 (2006) 372–92.

————. "Theology and Science: Where Are We?" *Zygon* 31 (1996) 323–43.

Pew Forum on Religion and Public Life. 2005 Survey: "Public Divided on Origins of Life." Online: http://harrisineractive.com/harris_poll/index.asp?PID=581.

Pigliucci, Massimo. *Denying Evolution: Creationism, Scientism, and the Nature of Science.* Sunderland, MA: Sinauer Associates, 2002.

Pius XII, Pope. *Humani Generis.* In *The Papal Encyclicals, 1939–1948,* edited by Claudia Carlen, I.H.M., 175–84. Raleigh, NC: McGrath, 1981.

Polkinghorne, John. *Traffic in Truth: Exchanges between Science and Theology.* Facets. Minneapolis: Fortress, 2002.

Rahner, Karl. "Evolution." In *Encyclopedia of Theology: The Concise Sacramentum Mundi,* edited by Karl Rahner, 475–88. New York: Seabury, 1975.

Religion / Newswriters. "Science: Evolution vs. Intelligent Design." Online: http://evolution.berkeley.edu/evolibrary/search/topicbrowse2.php?topic_id=47

Ruse, Michael. "Flawed Intelligence, Flawed Design: An Essay." *Virginia Quarterly Review* 82/2 (2006) 54–77.

Russell, Robert John, Nancey Murphy, and Arthur Peacocke, editors. *Chaos and Complexity: Scientific Perspectives on Divine Action.* Vatican City: Vatican Observatory, 1995. 2nd ed. 1997.

Russell, Robert John, Nancey Murphy, and C. J. Isham, editors. *Quantum Cosmology and the Laws of Nature: Scientific Perspectives on Divine Action.* Vatican City: Vatican Observatory, 1993. 2nd ed. 1996.

————, William Stoeger, and George V. Coyne, editors. *John Paul II on Science and Religion: Reflections on the New View from Rome.* Notre Dame: University of Notre Dame Press, 1990.

Sandeen, Ernest. *The Rise of Fundamentalism: British and American Millenarianism, 1990–1930.* Chicago: Chicago University Press, 1970.

Schüssler Fiorenza, Elisabeth. *Jesus—Miriam's Child, Sophia's Prophet: Critical Issues in Feminist Christology*. New York: Continuum, 1994.

Scott, Eugenie C. *Evolution vs. Creationism: An Introduction*. Berkeley: University of California Press, 2004.

————, and Glenn Branch. "Antievolutionism: Changes and Continuities." *BioScience* 53/3 (2003) 282–85.

Sharp, Doug. "Advice to Christians Who Must Deal with Evolutionists." Online: http://www.rae.org/advice/html.

Smith, Christopher Ralph. "Postmillennialism and the Work of Renewal in the Theology of Jonathan Edwards." Ph.D. dissertation, Boston College, 1992. Online: http://escholarship.bc.edu/dissertations/AAI9301702/.

Strimple, Robert B. "Was Adam an Historical Person? And What Difference Does It Make?" *Christian Renewal*, June 20, 1989. Online: www.wscal.edu/faculty/wscwritings/wasadamhistorical.php.

The Talk Origins Archive. "Exploring the Creation/Evolution Controversy." Online: http://www.talkorigins.org/.

Tammy Kitzmiller et al. v. Dover Area School District, Case 04cv2688, Judge Jones, December 20, 2005. Online: http://en.wikipedia.org/wiki/Kitzmiller_v._Dover_Area_School_District.

Theissen, Gerd, and Annette Merz. *The Historical Jesus: A Comprehensive Guide*. Translated by John Bowden. Minneapolis: Fortress, 1998.

Trible, Phyllis. "A Love Story Gone Awry?" In *God and the Rhetoric of Sexuality*, 72–143. Overtures to Biblical Theology. Philadelphia: Fortress, 1978.

University of California Museum of Paleontology. "Understanding Evolution." Online: http://evolution.berkeley.edu/.

————. "Evolution 101." Online: http://evolution.berkeley.edu/evolibrary/article/0_0_0/evo_01.

————. "How Does Evolution Impact My Life?" Online: http://evolution.berkeley.edu/evolibrary/search/topicbrowse2.php?topic_id=47.

————. "What Is Evolution and How Does It Work?" Online: http://evolution.berkeley.edu/evolibrary/search/topicbrowse2.php?topic_id=41.

————. "What Is the Evidence for Evolution?" Online: http://evolution.berkeley.edu/evolibrary/search/topicbrowse2.php?topic_id=46.

———. "What Is the History of Evolutionary Theory?" Online: http://evolution.berkeley.edu/evolibrary/search/topicbrowse2.php?topic_id=48.

Watts, Fraser. *Creation: Law and Probability*. Theology and the Sciences Series. Minneapolis: Fortress, 2008.

Way of Life Literature's Fundamental Baptist Information Service. "Genesis Is Literal History." Online: http://www.wayoflife.org/fbns/genesis-literal-history.html.

Welker, Michael. *Creation and Reality*. Minneapolis: Fortress, 1999.

Wells, Jonathan. *Icons of Evolution: Science or Myth? Why Much of What We Teach about Evolution Is Wrong*. Washington, DC: Regnery, 2000.

Whitcomb, J. C. Jr., and H. M. Morris. *The Genesis Flood*. Grand Rapids: Baker, 1961.

Wiley, Tatha. *Original Sin: Origins, Developments, Contemporary Meaning*. Mahweh, NJ: Paulist, 2002.

Zimmer, Carol. *E. Coli and the New Science of Life*. New York: Pantheon, 2008.